THE HIDDEN HELP

THE MYSTERIOUS WORK OF ANGELS IN THE BIBLE AND IN MY LIFE

THE HIDDEN HELP

THE MYSTERIOUS WORK OF ANGELS IN THE BIBLE AND IN MY LIFE

Jesse Duplantis

JESSE DUPLANTIS MINISTRIES

Destrehan, LA

DEDICATION

I would love to dedicate this book to the greatest miracle God has ever given to me and Cathy, and that is my daughter Jodi. Without Jodi's help in this ministry, I would've had a hard time accomplishing what I have accomplished. She has been such a blessing to me, and has researched things for me beyond what I could possibly ask or think. She's always told me, "Dad, you're the one with the original ideas." Yeah, but Jodi, you're the one who helped me put it all together. I can't thank you enough for who you are, can't thank you enough for being my daughter, but above all that, I can't thank you enough for your commitment, dedication, and discipline to this ministry and to your mom and I. I greatly appreciate you and everything that you do, and I want you to know without a shadow of a doubt that our life would be incomplete without you. This book is dedicated to you simply because you are YOU! There's nothing fake about you in any way, shape, or form. You say what you mean and mean what you say. To everyone reading this: I hope you enjoy this book because it could not have happened without the help of my daughter. I love you, Jodi!

The Hidden Help
© Copyright 2022—Jesse Duplantis

Published by Jesse Duplantis
PO Box 1089
Destrehan, LA 70047
www.jdm.org

Printed in the United States of America.

ISBN 13: 978-1-6341-6636-2

1 2 3 4 5 6 7 8 9 | 27 26 25 24 23 22

CONTENTS

"LET BROTHERLY LOVE CONTINUE.
BE NOT FORGETFUL
TO ENTERTAIN STRANGERS:
FOR THEREBY SOME
HAVE ENTERTAINED ANGELS
UNAWARES."

HEBREWS 13:1-2

INTRODUCTION

You have some Hidden Help. Angelic beings are real and many of them are here. That's right. They're not just in Heaven. They move between the worlds and dimensions God has created and can take on different forms. Hebrews 13:1-2 tells us there are times we can actually end up having contact and not even knowing it.

Some people seem to be aware of contact more than others. At times, some are given spiritual sight and insight—like a veil being pulled back between realms. Other times, it's not until after something takes place that you see the clues and realize you have *"entertained angels unawares,"* as Hebrews 13:2 says.

When I was young in the ministry, I was very hesitant to talk about some angelic experiences I had. I think whenever you talk about angels or anything that is outside of what people normally see and experience every day, there's always a risk of being thought of as some flaky Christian. The last thing I wanted to be known for was that when I was starting out, but at some point, I let go of that fear junk.

God's thoughts are higher than our thoughts and His ways are higher than ours, too (Isaiah 55:8-9)—and His angelic beings are proof of that! The situations we read about in the Bible reveal that what we see with the natural eye is just one side of a much bigger picture—a spiritual world that sounds crazy to the natural mind, but is, in fact, the way it really is.

Who cares if some people don't believe me when I tell what God did or showed to me? It has value to the ones it's meant to reach, and I believe that the Holy Spirit can take care of the timing, too. The Bible is full of supernatural experiences by people just like you and me, and all throughout, it reveals angelic intervention and visitation. In this book, I'll share a few of those biblical stories, some of my own personal experiences with angels, and some preaching and teaching, too.

I hope that when you finish this book, you'll know more than when you started. But, more than anything, I hope you are encouraged to know that this world isn't all there is, and that you are completely unique in God's creation. You're more valuable and loved than you can really comprehend. After all, two sides are warring just to have you. Your soul, your very being, is that valuable, and for good reason. More about that later!

Angels are here for a purpose. Some of those purposes the Word of God tells us. Others remain mysteries known only to God Almighty. That is the way it is, at least for now. You see, in this fallen world, we live as if we are looking through a glass darkly, but as the scripture says, one day all will be revealed. Until then, we live by faith and not by sight (2 Corinthians 5:7) We learn—we take that wisdom and knowledge and walk with God through the journey of life by faith in God. And we marvel at all His handiwork—whether it's this beautiful earth and the heavens we see, or the powerhouse angelic forces moving all around us just beyond the veil.

Angels are here for you, for others . . . but most of all, to make sure God's Word and God's will are fulfilled on the earth. Not one jot or tittle of what God said in His Word will be left undone (Matthew 5:18)—God will do exactly what He said, and guess what? On earth, in the heavens above, and in Heaven itself, angels are positioned to help make it happen! I hope you enjoy the book. May God bless you as you read it, and may you find wonder, peace, joy, and faith in God's wonderful angelic host and His perfect love for you.

CHAPTER 1

ALWAYS KEEP TWO TIRES ON THE SNOW

I had to get back to New Orleans. I was preaching in Crossett, Arkansas and the meeting was done, and I had a drive ahead of me. It was winter and freezing cold. There was snow coming from the sky and it was just bad. I had to get myself from Crossett to Monroe, Louisiana, because that was where I could catch a flight back to New Orleans. Back then, there was an airline called Republic Airlines, and they flew that route regularly. I was tired from preaching and not too excited to be driving in such bad weather.

Before I left that Assembly of God church, I remember the pastor saying, "Brother Jesse, it is snowing so bad and it's cold. You know how to drive in this kind of weather?" You see, he knew that I wasn't used to snow. I'm from South Louisiana and we rarely get snow. It's a freak event if we do. So, we just don't *know* how to drive in that kind of weather. We slip on a raindrop mixed with oil! So, you know snow and ice is just a recipe for hydroplaning. "Well, I'm gonna try to make it," I told him.

"Be careful of black ice," he told me, and I asked, "What does that mean?" "It's very slippery," he said and told me a little more. You see, I had no idea about such things back then. Well, we exchanged a few more words and said goodbye, and then I drove off into that weather.

By the time I hit about forty-five or so miles into my trip, I was driving in what was almost white-out conditions. I'm telling you, it was bad. I had the heater on full blast in that little rental car and I was still kind of cold. I was straining to just see the road, and I was driving pretty slowly. I'd made it to this long stretch of road that looked about two-miles long, and there was nothing but woods on both sides.

Well, just like that pastor had warned me, I hit some black ice—and when I did, the rental car started sliding sideways. I tried to correct the slide and thought I could because I wasn't going fast at all, but I had zero control, and as the car went sideways, I felt like it was speeding up. Before I knew it, it turned and sent me straight down this huge embankment toward the trees. That's when I hollered out, "Oh, Lord!!!!!" There was nothing I could do, and before I knew it, I was sliding into branches.

Now, I was only going maybe 35 mph, but it was still pretty scary going down like that. The branches were thick with packed snow, and all I could hear was pop-pop-pop as I slid down that embankment—the snow falling all over the car in clumps as the branches hit. Finally, I came to a stop, and when I did, I was thankful! I hadn't hit a tree directly head-on and that was great. What wasn't too great was that now I was off the road, down in an embankment and STUCK.

God, what I'm gonna do? I thought to myself. The black ice had gotten me, it was late and dark, and I was on a long stretch of wooded road in the middle of a snow storm. *Man, I guess I'm going to have to just sit here and let this engine keep running,* I thought to myself. So that's what I did . . . for about five minutes. It took that long for me to start feeling the cold setting in and to realize that the rental car's heater couldn't keep up with the cold outside the windows. So, I decided to get out and go back up to the road on foot.

I climbed up the embankment and looked both ways—and there was just nothing. It was quiet, still snowing, but black as an ace of spades with no good lighting on that road. With nothing and nobody around, I just didn't know what to do. All of a sudden, I saw a light and then two, and I realized somebody was coming. "That's a vehicle!" I said aloud.

It was a pickup truck with an old man behind the wheel. I was a lot younger then, but now that I think about it, he seemed to be about the age I am now. I didn't have to flag him down. He stopped on his own.

"Hey, young man, looks like you need some help."

"Yes, sir," I said, shivering in the cold.

"It's cold out here, isn't it?" he asked.

"Yes, sir," I said again.

He looked down the embankment and saw the rental and said, "Well, I got a chain in the back of this truck and I think I can get you out of there."

"Well, I certainly thank you," I said. We talked briefly, and then he got out and started getting the car all hooked up.

"Would you do me a favor?" he asked, "Get back in the car and when I pull on it, make sure your wheels are straight." So, I did and after a little bit, he pulled my rental straight out of the mud and snow, and I was back on the road.

I thought, *God, thank You, Jesus!*

We looked at each other and the car, and he said, "Well, the car's not damaged, and you're not damaged. You think you're gonna be all right?"

I said, "Yes, sir," again, and I told him thank you and just started to talk about the situation. "Man," I said, "I'm trying to get to Monroe, Louisiana to catch a flight in the morning . . ." You see, the service I'd preached that night had gone long. The Holy Spirit had been flowing, and after hanging out in the back with the pastor talking some more, I was really running a lot later than I'd wanted to.

So, I told him all about that and he said, "Well, I'm gonna give you some good wisdom. Make sure two wheels on the car stay on the snow side. In other words, drive two wheels on the shoulder, where the snow is. That'll give you traction."

"Remember," he said to me, "if you go to turn a curve like this and there's ice, you're just gonna slide down the curve, *Rrrrr*, and you're gonna start spinning again." I started to answer, but he interrupted me and said, "Do what I say, okay? And it'll help you."

"All right, thank you, sir! I'm from South Louisiana," I said, "You know, we don't have this kind of weather down there, not like this anyway."

He ended the conversation then with, "Well, you have a good day and . . . nice meeting you."

I said, "Is there anything I can do, to pay you . . . something?"

"Oh, no," he said and smiled at me, "this is what I do." I thought that was a strange thing to say, so I nodded and put my car in drive. But before I could even roll, I thought, *No, I gotta give that guy something*! So, I put the car back into park. It had only been maybe 20 seconds since I'd heard the last words he ever said to me . . . but when I opened my door to get out, he was gone. His truck was gone. And there were NO lights on the road.

Like I said, that stretch of road was a good two-miles long and straight as an arrow. I looked down one way and then the next. I couldn't believe my eyes. It was silent. The snow was still falling . . . and there was no truck, no man, no tail lights, and no . . . well, nothing! I was alone again. I couldn't help myself,

"Good God!" I said aloud standing in that street. And I remembered suddenly that scripture from Hebrews 13:2, ". . . *some have entertained angels unawares.*"

"I just entertained an angel unawares," I told myself. "The angel said to keep two tires on the snow," I said aloud to myself and laughed.

I got back into that car in sheer amazement, and I slowly drove to Monroe, Louisiana, just like he said, and caught my early flight back to New Orleans International Airport.

Angels, like the one who helped me on that snowy road, are what I call *The Hidden Help*. They remain unseen to us, working in the spirit realm mostly, but they can also take on human form and walk amongst us. They can change their appearance at will. They can adopt a human look if they are on assignment to intervene or interact with us in some way. Sometimes, when they do this, it seems like they purposefully leave clues for us to notice after-the-fact. They did this in biblical times, and they still do it today.

"Let brotherly love continue. Be not forgetful to entertain strangers: for thereby some have entertained angels unawares."
HEBREWS 13:1-2

This verse is a reminder that God's angels don't stay in Heaven. Many are here on earth and go back and forth between the spirit world we cannot see and the natural world we can see. God always has angels on assignment. I believe they help us more than we even know. They see what is going on in a way that we can't, and they move according to the will and Word of God. The more we speak God's Word, the more they listen and attend—because they were created to serve Him.

These mysterious angelic servants of God are a blessing. They're just one more way God gets things done, whether it's on the earth, the heavens, or in Heaven itself. And I really do believe, just like Hebrews 13:1-2 says, that we should make living in brotherly love a habit and treat the strangers we encounter in life (along with those we already know) with goodness, generosity, and a heart to do right. After all, we really don't know who we're talking to some days. We don't know at all! That stranger helping you in a pinch? That stranger asking for help from you? Well, they might not be what you think they are. They just might be on assignment to you.

CHAPTER 2

BROTHERLY LOVE AND ANGELS IN DISGUISE

God's Word says, *"Let brotherly love continue"* before we are told to *"Be not forgetful to entertain strangers: for thereby some have entertained angels unawares"* in Hebrews 13:1-2. That's because how we treat others is important to God. In this verse, God's Word links brotherly love and angelic visitation. Remember that.

How we treat others is a reflection on nobody but us. We're called to do right and be a reflection *of* Christ in this world; not cast a reflection *upon* Christ. The only Jesus some people will ever see is the Jesus in you or the Jesus in me—you've probably heard me say that if you've ever heard me preach. It means that witnessing for Jesus is about sharing the Gospel message, but it's also about letting your light shine and being the message by doing what God says to do.

God *is* love. That means He wants us to be loving. We access love through the gift He gave us—the love He shed abroad in our heart upon salvation. You see, when we get saved, we get love. It's a deposit God makes into our heart. When the sin falls away, when the redemption comes, the love naturally bubbles up. It's only when we let the pressures of the world, the fears of our mind, or the issues of our heart take over that we find ourselves *not* acting in love towards others.

Sometimes we will miss it, but, if or when we do miss it, it's important that we notice it, repent to God, and start treating others again as if they were personally sent from God to shine a light on our character. *"Let brotherly love continue"* needs to be a part of our everyday life, and not just something we do at church or when we think somebody's watching. Somebody is ALWAYS watching! God and all the spiritual forces, good and bad, see us as we go through this earthly experience. Remember that, too.

I want you to notice that Hebrews 13:2 specifically mentions *strangers* after talking about *brotherly love*. We shouldn't ignore people as we go about our day. We're not in this world just to do what *we* want to do 24/7. The spiritual reality is that God has angels on this earth that deliberately take on human form to interact with us—and that's why God's Word warns us to *"Be not forgetful"* to act right with strangers, because we never really know who we're talking to!

Angels in disguise is a phenomenon that's been going on since the beginning of time. The Hidden Help don't just intervene in situations, they also take on forms of people in everyday life. That's right! How else do you think you could encounter an angel and not know it? They can change their appearance and look like someone you'd never think they never would. Sometimes your spirit might be so sensitive that you recognize them in the moment. Other times you may find yourself rushing through your day and completely unaware . . . until it's too late.

Years ago, I was just going to eat at Mr. B's, my favorite restaurant in the French Quarter section of New Orleans. If you've ever been to the French Quarter, you know that the streets are narrow and it's hard to find a parking spot on the street. I don't like parking on the street anyway, so I always go into a parking garage. So, that day, I'd just parked and I was walking out onto the street, going fast to get to where I wanted to go.

Rushing can make you act differently than if you weren't rushing, and that day I made a total mistake that I have regretted ever since. I was busy, I had to fly out that afternoon, but there was some furniture I wanted to go look at in downtown New Orleans. So, instead of going another day, I decided I'd just go quickly while I was already down there. I was planning on looking fast, making a decision on it, and eating lunch at my favorite place before I flew out.

Now, I've never forgotten this and it hurts me to this day when I think about it—and while I wouldn't call it a sin, it was wrong. My heart was so grieved afterwards; I thought I'd share my mistake in this book—because even though I'm a preacher, I definitely don't always get things right.

As I was walking up the street, all I could think about was getting to that dumb furniture store and getting in and out. I was bee-lining it up the street when this man came up to me and stopped me, and he was all disheveled. He had the look of a homeless man, but one of the worst I've seen. He was dirty and messy looking, but when I looked into his face, even as quick as I did, I could tell something was different about him.

I was in a hurry and he was distracting me from what I wanted to do, and I felt irritated. I could tell he wanted something from me before he even spoke. He said, "Could you help me? I'm hungry. Could you help me?"

Now, I saw his long, thin, scraggly hair. I saw his dirty clothes. But I was so impatient and in a rush; I tried to ignore it. What I couldn't ignore was the look in his eyes. It was the most hopeless I'd ever seen a person look—and I've seen broken people, homeless people, and all sorts of people at the end of their rope. But this man's hopelessness was different. It was so deep; I've never seen anyone with that look since.

Still, I was rushing. I thought I'd just come back to him after the furniture store, and so I said, "Sir, I can't . . . Listen, I'll help you, but just give me a minute here. I've got to run over and do this thing." I saw the sadness in his eyes, but I said, "I'll be back." I just ignored that sadness and started to walk fast. Now, I was about 20 feet to the corner of the street where I was walking on Royal Street—and I walked for mere seconds when I thought to myself, *All you have to do is give the guy some money or something to help.* So, I turned around to go back to the man.

Now, there was no way from where he was that he could have walked fast enough to get to the next corner in those few seconds that passed before I turned around. There was no way he could've stepped into an alley because there is no alley there. There was no way he could've crossed the street; I'd have seen him walking and doing it. He couldn't go anywhere in that amount of time. There was a truck on the road and it was still there, I could see. He couldn't have gotten into the truck without me seeing, and he wasn't in the truck. That man was GONE.

When I say he was gone, I mean he vanished. He wasn't on the sidewalk, on the street, in the truck . . . he was nowhere. I stood there looking in every direction and there was nowhere he could go in that time, and yet he was gone. It was impossible for him to be and I knew it. In my mind, I saw his eyes again—that deep, utter hopelessness—and that's when I felt a tap in my spirit and I just *knew*.

I'm telling you, my heart sank inside my chest. Inside myself, I said, *Oh, God, that was an angel. That was an angel trying to teach me something, but I was too busy.* I knew when I had looked in his eyes that he was different; I could see it. I just was too focused on my plan for the day and too busy to stop . . . and it bothers me even to this day. I should've helped in that instant on the street that day. I knew in my spirit I should have paused and realized that that person was more important than my plan. It would have taken me seconds to help him, but I didn't even do that.

I knew right then and there that I didn't pass the test, for lack of a better way to say it. I had some growing up in Christ to do, and in that moment, I saw how much. Right there on the street, standing where he had been, I bowed my head and said aloud, "God, forgive me!" I felt so bad, I can't even tell you how bad I felt inside. That sinking feeling when you know you've missed the mark.

"I already did," God said to my spirit, "Thank you." That's all He said to me.

You see, we all mess up. Sometimes we don't do the right thing when confronted with the option. But when we realize our error, we need to be quick to admit it. We need to be quick to repent. That's the only way we're ever going to get better. Admitting your error and repenting is the first step to learning a good life lesson, which can help you to do right in the moment more often in the future. Sometimes it hurts us to see where we fail, but if we learn from it, we will be much more aware not to do it again.

I've never forgotten that day, and I never will as long as I ever live. It touches me when I think about it—that God would send someone like that, looking like that, giving me a spiritual clue in the eyes even, just to help me learn where I was weak. You see, that angel may have asked *me* for help to see what I'd do, but in not doing what I should have, *I'm* the one who was really helped. That's how I look at it because it taught me something. It made me say to myself, "I will never do that again as long as I ever live. God, forgive me."

To me, that is one of the greatest angelic experiences I've ever had—because it changed me. For many years I'd replay that day in my mind. I'd imagine myself doing something different. I'd imagine myself acting fast to help him instead of being fast to try and stick to my plan. I'd think, *What would that angel have done if I'd just stopped, given him money, and prayed with him too?* I like to think he'd have lit up like a light . . . because I'd never seen so much hopelessness. I don't beat myself up over it anymore, but I don't let it slide out of my memory either, like it's unimportant. Nothing God does to teach us something about ourselves is unimportant, whether He uses the Hidden Help or not.

We should never be in such a hurry that we miss out on the opportunities God sends our way to help others that come directly across our path. I missed it that day, yes, but I'd like to think I've gained more sensitivity just by the experience. That's all God wanted of me, really. That's what He wants from all of us—brotherly love that isn't too distracted to notice when somebody needs us.

I believe that God wanted me to see that my impatience can cause me to miss things if I'm not careful. He wanted me to see that faith and hurry don't mix well for me—and that all I need to do is pause long enough to help when He asks me to help. That's being instant in season and out of season (2 Timothy 4:2). That's doing the right thing. It's about being available for whatever God puts on the path of our life.

I've got to tell you . . . I'm still looking for that angel, hahaha! When I get to Heaven, I want to meet the one who was given that assignment. He was my very own Hidden Help that day on Royal Street in New Orleans—and like I said, that's one of the greatest angelic experiences I've ever had in life.

The Hidden Help have all sorts of assignments concerning us, and every one of them help us in some way—even if it is just to shine a light on an area in our life that we need to grow more in Christ. Do you think God knew beforehand that I'd fail the test? Of course He did. That's why He sent the angel! Did my own "missing it" teach me something that I've never forgotten? YES! It did.

When I look back, I can see God was giving me a clue right in that man's eyes. This world is tough, and even Christians sometimes are too busy in their own world to bother with some people God puts on our path—but it doesn't matter what we're doing, if we don't walk in brotherly love, we're missing it.

We can't see the Hidden Help unless they manifest in some way to our natural eyes, but we know through the scriptures that there are some who are always here. They were here on this earth before we were and, as servants of God, we have to realize that they do not only do dramatic things. They also serve God in very small ways—ways that help to make us more aware of the importance of brotherly love.

The Hidden Help have been helping people since the beginning in one way or another. They can't *make* us do anything, though—we have been given free will by God. But these servants of God can give us opportunities to do right, and the question is, will we take it when it comes? Will we make a habit of doing the right thing so much in our daily life that even if an angel shows up, we can pass the test?

Angels in disguise don't always show up when the time is "right" for us. They move according to God's Word and God's will, period. And that means any and every lesson they help us to learn is important. When we get to Heaven, I believe we will know just how many angels came across our path. I believe we'll find out if we passed or failed the moments we were given to show love. So, let's do what the Hebrews 13:1-2 says and *"Let brotherly love continue."* Let's *"Be not forgetful to entertain strangers: for thereby some have entertained angels unawares."*

CHAPTER 3

ANGELS EXIST TO SERVE GOD

Angels could be anywhere they want to be. The faithful ones that didn't fall with Satan remain true to the Father— they only follow God's Word and God's will. The word *angel* means "messenger" in both Hebrew and Greek, because the angels here have been given the duty to be messengers for God. They visit God's people to deliver words from God. They help to move God's will and the Church forward from behind the scenes. They warn God's people of danger. They save God's people from situations they don't even realize are about to happen. Some are positioned in certain places in the world. Some are assigned to individual people. They do all sorts of things, and many things we simply do not know. They're most often hidden, unless God wills that they reveal themselves.

The angels of God can take on human forms to look like us or reveal themselves exactly how they were originally created by

God—materializing in and out of our sight at God's will (Genesis 19:1-3, Hebrews 13:2, Revelation 10:1-3). Angels were part of our Creation (Genesis 2:1, Job 38:1,4,7; Colossians 1:16, Jude 6). There are many here and, like always, they continue to assist God. They are supernatural beings, and along with supernatural strength and abilities, they also have great discernment and wisdom (2 Samuel 14:17,20).

Angels can and will do completely impossible things in order to fulfill God's sovereign plan. They will be major players in the end times, too. They'll be with us to the end of the world and beyond. God's angels are powerful beings with incredible capabilities and great intelligence—and they are holy and sinless before God.

So, why would these heavenly angels *help* us? Why would these beings, capable of so much, even *speak* to us? Why would they have *anything* to do with us humans here on earth at all? There's only one reason: GOD. The faithful ones do what God wants done. They aren't just carriers of messages for God, but they take on varying rolls to advance the Church.

In the Bible, when angels didn't take on a human form to interact with someone—when they revealed themselves in their own form—they shocked the socks off of people! When they appear as themselves, they are flat overwhelming to our natural eyes. There's a reason they had to say, "Fear not!" to so many people in the Word. Being scared is a pretty natural reaction. We're just not used to seeing huge, bright, lit-up-like-the-sun beings speaking the Word and will of God.

These beings have power and ability beyond what we yet know. All we know is what God's Word says. Beyond that, the details of how they were made, how long they've been in existence, or what each and every one is capable of is just plain unknowable. What we do know is that God created them all to *serve* in one way or another—I want you to really understand that. No matter how majestic, no matter how powerful, and no matter how extraordinary we think they are, God created them to serve.

We serve too, but God created us for a different purpose than the angels. We were created to be God's *family*. God loves us and considers us like children. We are something special to the Father. A unique triune creation made in His image and likeness. A mix of the dust of the earth and the breath of Almighty God. We aren't like the angels. We are sons and daughters who serve, and in the order of His creation, that makes us *different*.

From the dust our bodies were made, but from the breath of God we were given life. One breath set this all into motion. One blast of breath from God and we began. That breath made us eternal spirit-beings, housed in temporary, corruptible mortal flesh—and, apparently, that combination is unique in all of creation . . . and very, very precious to God. So, we are fragile by comparison to the angels, weaker physically, and learning as we go in life, but because we are God's family, we are favored even above the highest of angelic beings. Still, we are all working together and unified with the angels under this: We ALL love and serve God, and we know He deserves all the glory and praise. God loves us, and we are distinct in His creation.

Love. That's not just what God does; it's Who He *is*. God *is* love. He is also holy beyond our comprehension—pure, holy, and both merciful and just. The angels He created? They are in awe of Him. They reverence Him. They exist to serve Him, and they do it with true honor and often joy, which makes them break out into praise or song. The angels defer to God and speak of Him in glowing terms. Angels also speak on behalf of God to us with a capacity for duty we can't grasp. They're not human. Their capacity for dutifulness seems to be on a whole other level. It's just how they were made. More than anything, they know they were made to do the works of God and serve His will.

Powerful servants. Powerful messengers. Powerful supernatural beings that innately know that *we* are favored by God and called His children. We are what God created us to be: His *family*. You see, we weren't created to just be servants. We were created to be sons and daughters who serve. There's a difference! Even in our fragility, the angels recognize us as different to God and higher ranking than they are.

We're always going to be kids. Really, you can think of it like that. God never calls us His adults. He calls us His children. And what do children need? They need guidance. They need instruction. They need help! As servants of God, as beings who do what God loves, they choose to obey the Father when it comes to us. You see, the angels have seen God in a way we have not seen Him yet—in all His glory and power. They *know* there is nothing and no one above God.

So, if God Himself calls *us* His sons and His daughters, if He has created *us* to be His family, then the angels know it, too. The faithful angelic beings know it. The fallen angelic beings know it. Everything in Heaven and in hell knows it.

You've got to ask yourself if *you* know it.

There's an epidemic in this world of people walking around with no clue of who and Whose they are—but I have a feeling that if you're reading this book, you have a clue! The angels have no such dilemma when it comes to us. Like I said, they *know!* So they offer help to us from time to time, and likely more than we will ever know until we get to Heaven, because they *know.* They know we're children caught in the crosshairs of a war that started in Heaven when Satan wanted to be like God and rebelled. They know we'll continue being in the middle of that war until Jesus comes.

Angelic beings also know that once we accept Christ, once we are forgiven and are made righteous through Jesus' sacrifice on the cross, we are children with immense power—because with salvation through Christ, we get authority. God gave us the power to use His name and His Word to defeat anything that rises up against us, even angels in rebellion. It's almost funny that we, as children of God, can stand up to and defeat fallen angelic beings simply with our faith in God, His name, and His Word.

When believers don't know that God made them His family, when they don't realize their position and authority in Christ, they can easily feel as if supernatural beings have a higher position with God than they do. The reality is that angels do not have a higher position than the children of God. If they were to be confronted with something so jaw-dropping as an angel, they just might do something crazy like fall on their face in praise of them. Let me tell you something, praising angels is totally against the Word of God. We must *always* put God first over anything He's made, whether natural or supernatural.

God alone is worthy of our praise. After all, *everything* was created by Him and *everything* is held together by Him (Colossians 1:13-17). And we are specifically told *not* to worship angels in the Bible. We can never forget that God is the head of everything. God holds the Body of Christ together, not signs, wonders, visions, or angels. God is the Head, not His created beings (Colossians 2:18-19). So, when thinking about angelic beings or even if we have experiences with them, we have to remember that God's angels assist Him and help or give messages on *His* behalf.

The faithful angelic beings *always* point us to God— the Father, the Son, and the Holy Spirit—they *never* go against His Word or His will. If they intervene in the life of a human being, it's just because they know God wants it done. Period. That's because the Hidden Help and every other angelic being have been created to serve God's will, not their own will—or ours, unless our will lines up with God's will. God's Word is His will. That's why it's so important for us to fill our mind and heart with the Word of God. If we are speaking the Word and our will is in line with it, then God's angels help us—but they are under no obligation to help us if we aren't.

So, if you ever do happen to see an angel manifested and have a knee-jerk reaction to praise them, they will let you know quick, fast, and in a hurry to stop doing it. The faithful ones will refuse to allow you to take them out of their God-given position. They will correct and redirect all your praise to God. They will not accept your praise. They will not step out of God's created divine order.

If you think you'd never fall for praising an angel, think again. In the book of Revelation, the apostle John was having vision after vision, and they were coming to him from an angel on God's behalf—and it overwhelmed him so much, even he messed up and fell into worship. Read how he puts it. *"Now I, John, saw and heard these things. And when I heard and saw, I fell down to worship before the feet of the angel who showed me these things. Then he said to me, 'See that you do not do that. For I am your fellow servant, and your brethren the prophets, and of those who keep the words of this book. Worship God'"* (Revelation 22:8-9 NKJV). Notice how the angel stops John, and quick! Notice how the angel tries to get it across to John that they are in it together, and that he is not above John or God.

If an angel *does* accept your praise and even tries to illicit more of it from you, well . . . that's how you know you aren't dealing with the faithful. You're being deceived by the fallen.

Those angels follow Satan, and they're prideful just like he is. Satan rebelled because he wanted to be like God—he wanted glory and praise. The fallen ones want it, too. They're quick to let you do it, and feed lies to give you even more reasons to praise them. They lie all the time, sometimes using truth and twisting it, and their only loyalty is to themselves—if they talk about God at all, they will twist His words and lie some more. They're masters of deception.

The angels of God are pure and are fiercely loyal to Him. They understand their position and are thrilled to be in it—and they love the pure words of God. The faithful ones aren't prideful. Only a fallen angel would let you keep praising him and giving him the thanks that belongs to God. Remember that. The Word tells us they can take on the form of an angel of light (2 Corinthians 11:13-15). Don't let their fake light fool you. In the last days, some will do that—they'll be influenced by the fallen. The Word says some will end up following the doctrines of demons (1 Timothy 4:1). As they say, all that glitters is not gold.

All praise and glory belong to God alone—I can't emphasize that enough. God is our supreme Creator; not the angels who help Him, no matter how magnificent they are. Even today, some well-meaning people claim they've been told by beings from the heavens that *they* created everything we see. That means those beings are claiming to do what God said *He* did. That's called deception.

If God said He created this world, then He did. If angels contradict God, they are trying to deceive mankind, and they lie because they are the fallen. They are in league with the author of lies himself, Satan—and just remember that the reason he fell in the first place was because he wanted to be like God (Isaiah 14:12-14). So, it's no big shock that he wants to take credit for what he didn't create. He's a liar and a thief who comes to steal, kill, and destroy. Anything he says that seems "good" is just being used to deceive you, because twisting the truth is what he does. He's wicked, and that means twisted.

I'll get to more about Satan later, but just remember that God's Word tells us that even if a being shows up like "an angel of light," if they deny Christ, they are not good and not God's! They are just lying, stinking, fallen angels and demons trying to deceive you with a fake cloak of bright light and words that make you feel good.

So, don't be fooled by false light. Don't be led astray by anything that does not recognize Jesus as Messiah, God's Son, and point you to salvation from sin by His sacrifice on the cross. Jesus is the Way, the Truth, and the Life—nobody's getting to the Father unless they go through Him, no matter how much they rationalize their erroneous thinking. They can look good and sound good and still be pushing totally false doctrines that have nothing to do with God.

Don't let that scare you off from admiring God's faithful angels, though. God wouldn't have allowed us to know about them if He wanted us to ignore them completely! He wouldn't send them if He didn't want us to know them or even meet them. Angelic beings are wonderful creations of God—a species apart from us, but still united with us in love for God and all He says and does.

As long as you don't praise them, you are doing nothing wrong by learning about them and admiring them for their role in God's work—because they are totally worthy of that! I love the world God created—the people, the animals, and all of nature is magnificent to me. I don't feel guilty admiring any of it. I don't feel guilty praising God for any of it either. I hope you get my point.

I believe God enjoys it when we think what He made is wonderful. I think He just loves when we admire what He's done—because it blesses Him to please us with the work of His hands. God creates beautiful things, astounding things, and He creates majestic beings of all sorts, too. The angels are God's handiwork, and they're worth being amazed by. All you have to do is avoid putting anything, including God's creations, above *Him*. That's it. And that's easy!

CHAPTER 4

THE ANGEL AND THE STONE: TURNING PROBLEMS INTO PULPITS

I was on a plane flying to a meeting one day when I got a revelation just reading about an angel in the Word. There I was, just reading Matthew's account of Jesus' resurrection, and all of a sudden, I saw the most astounding thing. It was something I'd missed every time I'd read that old, familiar scripture. Yet there it was in black and white. In addition to redemption from sin, Satan, death, hell, and the grave, the Lord suddenly painted me a clear picture of how I could be redeemed from my own problems right then and there—by acting just like the angel at the empty tomb.

God showed me that what that angel did was turn a problem into a pulpit. In that one miraculous story, it suddenly dawned on me that what that angel did was an open display of Satan's defeat . . . and it was an example of what I, and every other believer, could do when confronted with problems in life, too.

Now, I've learned to never elevate the problems over the promises. I've learned to put what God did above anything the devil did or is doing in my life. I believe and preach that no matter how large a problem is, there's no reason to mentally make them into "stones" that we can't move because nothing is impossible with God! The crucifixion, death, and victorious resurrection of Jesus Christ show us that. His victory over hell, death, and the grave was the most life-changing event that has ever happened.

Just thinking about that empty tomb gets me excited! Every time I read through Matthew and get to the part where those women go to the tomb to lay spices on Jesus' body and find the stone rolled away, I want to shout, "He's risen!" at the top of my lungs. You see, Jesus didn't stay on the cross, and the devil couldn't keep Him in the tomb. He beat Satan and all his works—all the works he and his demon fallen angels do—in three days. I want you to read this passage about the empty tomb and let it paint a picture for you:

> Now after the Sabbath, as it began to dawn toward the first day of the week, Mary Magdalene and the other Mary came to look at the grave.
>
> And behold, a severe earthquake had occurred, for an angel of the Lord descended from Heaven and came and rolled away the stone and _sat_ upon it.
>
> And his appearance was like lightning, and his clothing as white as snow.
>
> The guards shook for fear of him and became like dead men.
>
> The angel said to the women, 'Do not be afraid; for I know that you are looking for Jesus who has been crucified.
>
> 'He is not here, for He has risen, just as He said. Come, see the place where He was lying.
>
> 'Go quickly and tell His disciples that He has risen from the dead; and behold, He is going ahead of you into Galilee, there you will see Him; behold, I have told you.'
>
> MATTHEW 28:1-7 NASB1995

That day, as I was sitting on the plane reading this passage, the Spirit of God spoke to me and said, "Jesse, My angel sat upon the obstruction that was holding Jesus in the tomb." I unbuckled my seat belt and jumped up shouting, "The angel sat on the stone!" A man across the aisle looked at me real strange. "Hey!" I said to him, "The angel sat on the stone!" He just said, "Okay . . ." like he didn't want to talk, hahaha. "Look here," I said, pointing at the scripture, "the devil tried to hold Jesus in the grave, but God sent an angel to knock the stone away. It caused an earthquake, and then the angel sat on the stone!"

I danced a little charismatic hop. That man thought I was crazy. But it had dawned on me that if the angel of the Lord sat on the problem, that's exactly what I should do. If the angel of the Lord used that obstruction as a place to kick back and proclaim the Good News, then that's what you and I are supposed to do, too! We need to realize that what Satan used to hold Jesus *in* is what was used by that angel to proclaim that Jesus was *out*. Hallelujah! I get excited just thinking about it today.

Do you see it? Do you have a picture of it in your mind, like I did? I hope you do, because this little revelation really changed things for me. What is amazing to me is that the devil had guards around the tomb. They were guarding a dead man! When was the last time you saw that happen? Well, if you've got even a small part of the power of God, the devil is afraid of you. When God blew Jesus out of the tomb, those devils bit the dust, and so did the guards!

Everybody has problems. The devil makes sure that all of us have a stone or two. There's nothing unique or new about that. But, sadly, instead of rolling the stone away and using it as a place to sit and testify, many people canonize their stone. They try to make it holy. "Would you like to see my tumor?" they ask as they begin to compare the size of theirs with others.

Satan has marked and branded many of the Body of Christ today. We can all see that plainly. But Jesus never said that we were supposed to bear the marks of Satan. He told us that we are to bear the marks of a Christian (Galatians 6:17 NKJV). And the marks of a Christian are not sickness, disease, lack, or misery. Those things are from Satan, designed to keep us entombed and forever bound.

Today you may be looking at a big obstacle blocking your way. If you are, it is time you quit crying and start doing something about it. Weeping at the foot of the obstacle won't move it an inch. Talking about how bad it is won't roll it away any quicker. There is no reason why you have to stay bound by a stone carved in hell. You can use the Word of God to roll that stone away!

The Word is powerful enough to miraculously move that stone. All you've got to do is believe it. And once you do, then you can park yourself on top of what was designed to hold you back and begin to proclaim your freedom in Jesus. Just like in the Bible, you can sit on what the devil meant to hold you in with and proclaim that you are now out. Glory!

Remember, you can't have a testimony until you have a test. So, shout! You've got an opportunity to use your faith and trample on the devil. I want you to know something. Jesus said He was coming for a Church without spot or wrinkle—and that only happens when we are saved and washed through His blood, because on our own we cannot wash away iniquity. The more we lean on the blood and the less we give in to the temptation of the devil to stay stuck in the "tomb" of our problem, the more we can live free.

Freedom starts in the heart with the acceptance of Jesus Christ, but it continues in the way we live our life. Are we going to have faith or are we going to live in doubt? Are we going to use the Word or are we going to accept everything Satan does as just "part of life"? No! In Christ we have the power to not only overcome, but to also make an open display of Satan's defeat by making every problem a pulpit of sorts—we do not have to stay stuck when Jesus died to set us free.

It's time for us to learn to sit on our problems. It's time to sit on that alcohol or drug habit instead of partaking in it. Spend time with God and let His glory come out of your inner man like lightning. It'll consume that thing. The stone that covered the opening of Jesus' tomb was Satan's attempt to throw an obstacle in God's path. What should you do with the obstacle that Satan puts in the way of your miracle? Climb up on it and use it as a pulpit to proclaim the Gospel.

Have you got a problem? Then, bless God, you've got a pulpit! If you've got cancer, climb up on that thing and declare the Gospel: "Jesus took my infirmity. He bore my sickness. And by the stripes on His back, I am healed!" (Isaiah 53:4-5). Turn the tables on the devil. Take the thing he meant to use to destroy you and turn it to glorify God.

Do you remember what the scripture says the prince of this world, the devil, thought of after Jesus was crucified and he'd realized what he'd done? First Corinthians 2:8 (NKJV) says, *"Which none of the princes of this world knew: for had they known it, they would not have crucified the Lord of glory."* Had the devil known, he would have never killed Jesus! When you start beating the devil at every turn, he'll start saying the same thing about YOU!

You can beat the devil up so much that you get to the place where he says, "Man, if I would have only known, I wouldn't have put that cancer on him. Now look at him! He's telling everybody how he got healed." Or maybe he will say, "Man, if I would have only known, I wouldn't have tried to destroy her marriage because, look! Now she's telling everyone how Jesus healed her marriage." You've got to believe it and climb up on that stone with gusto. That's the way to overcome!

Give me a problem and I'll have a pulpit. I love to confuse the devil. I've learned to inject thoughts into his mind. It knocks his socks off. Why would I do that? Why would I encourage you to do the same? Well, he throws thoughts into your mind often enough, doesn't he? Don't you think it's time you threw a few into his?! The Bible gives us instructions on how to combat thoughts that don't line up with the Word.

The Bible tells us in 2 Corinthians 10:5 to bring every thought into captivity to the obedience of Christ. And if we don't want the devil to get a foothold in our lives, then it is critical that we do that. But I've learned how to really irritate the devil. When he throws a thought into my mind, I don't care if I'm standing in a crowd, I'm going to deliberately think a faith thought. And he knows what I'm doing because I let him know! "I'm going to preach the Word of God and get everybody saved!" First, I think it, and then I say it!

I know how to irritate the devil. My radar is up, and if he's anywhere near, I'll know it. The devil will be afraid for me to get up tomorrow morning. He doesn't know what I'm going to do. I'll get up in the morning and put a "behold" on myself. I'll say what 2 Corinthians 5:17 says, *"Therefore if any man be in Christ, he is a new creature: old things are passed away; behold [Jesse], all things are become new."*

"Oh yeah, Brother Jesse, but my problem is so hard. I can't just say something and make it go away. I'm fat. I can't help it. My Mama's fat. My Uncle Fred is fat. My Uncle Fred's dog is fat. We're all just fat!"

Have you ever taken the time to stop and realize that your body was made by the Lord and He can help you to overcome any obstacle that's weighing it down? I know food has a voice. It does! And it'll talk to you if you'll listen. Food has talked to me many times. Once, when I was at lunch with someone who ordered chocolate mousse for dessert, it seemed to know my name. "Pssst, Jesse! Reach your spoon over here."

Now at the time, I was watching what I was eating when that chocolate started talking to me. I'd already decided that I was working on something with my body. Today, I have no problem with any food. I eat whatever I want, just less of it. But back then, when the chocolate came, I was learning self-control and was on a specific diet. I was buffeting my flesh, so to speak.

So, what did I do when the chocolate wouldn't shut up? I rebuked that thing in the name of Jesus, resisted that temptation—and soon, guess what? The devil fled! Hahaha, that's a joke, but I'm telling you, if you struggle with food like I did for years, sometimes you have to tell food to "Shut up!" What good will that do? It will cause you to climb upon that obstacle—it will help you see yourself as in authority over your own body, and not the other way around.

Sometimes you have to roll the stone away and sit on it, and proclaim that you have the victory over what has been trying to keep you down, and maybe even hidden for years. Whatever your struggle, whatever your problem, don't elevate it. No matter how large they may appear, don't make them out to be stones you can't move—because you can. From big to little things, you are more than a conqueror through Christ Jesus (Romans 8:37). And those stones have got to move by the power of His name!

"But, Brother Jesse, I can't stop drinking."

Yes, you can.

"But, Brother Jesse, I can't lose this weight."

Yes, you can.

"But, Brother Jesse, I can't quit committing fornication."

Yes, you can.

"But how?"

Sit on them! Get up on that obstacle and start proclaiming your victory in faith. And then, when the devil tries to get you to doubt God's Word is true, doubt it! Quit lying to yourself! When you say, "Oh, I can't," you are elevating the obstacle instead of sitting on it. You may not *want* to quit, but you *can* quit. You may not want to quit drinking, but you can. You might not want to treat your body like a temple instead of a trashcan, but you can. It is all a decision. You choose what you are going to do. Nobody but you!

That may be hard to hear, but it's the truth. And if you'll take your mind off that trash and fill it with the Spirit of the living God, you will roll that stone away. And once you do, you'll find that you can't help but sit on it and proclaim what the Lord has done in you.

I agree with what I once heard Charles Capps say, "Doubt your doubts!"

I was flying on a little commuter plane one time and the woman next to me started sneezing. "It looks as if you've got a cold." I said.

"Yeah."

"Do you believe in healing?"

"Uh, well, our pastor talks about it."

"Okay," I said, "bow your head."

"Here?"

"Well, do you want to cough all the way and spread those germs all over everybody, or do you want a healing?"

"Uh . . . well . . ."

"Don't worry," I said, "people will get quiet."

Then I turned around and announced, "Y'all calm down! We're gonna pray for this woman's healing!"

I laid my hands on her shoulder and prayed, "Father, in Jesus' name, I rebuke the virus that's trying to invade her body. We invade her body with Holy Ghost cells of power, dominion, and authority!" A guy who was drinking nearby went, "Whoa!" But that woman needed some help doubting her doubts. I just used her obstacle as a pulpit to proclaim God's goodness.

I was in an airport another time when I saw a man having a fit of carnality over the hot dog machine. He put his money in the machine, but he didn't get the hot dog. He started screaming, cussing, and punching the machine.

"Give me my hot dog!"

Bam! Bam! He started hitting the glass. I thought it was pretty stupid, and I figured what he really needed to do was sit on his problem. So, I strolled over.

"What's the matter, Sir?"

He called the machine a few choice words before he said, "It won't give me my hot dog!"

"Well, did you pray for it?"

He looked at me like I was insane.

"I'm gonna pray for this machine to give you your hot dog." I said. You can laugh if you want to, but that man needed Jesus! Anybody cussing and punching a vending machine in the airport needs God! I felt like an idiot as I laid my hands on that machine.

The devil started harassing me with doubting thoughts, *Suppose the weenie don't come out?* I grabbed the machine. "Devil," I commanded, "turn loose of that weenie! Turn loose of the thing in the name of Jesus!" *Plop!* The hot dog fell out, just like that. A hippie dude walked over to me. "Say, brother, can you get me one?"

"No, he paid for his. You have to pay for yours." I should have prayed for chili and mustard on it, too. That would have been a miracle! Still, I just used that machine as a pulpit to proclaim the Good News of the Gospel.

If you will move off the humorous side of the situation, you will see there are people entombed with terrible problems and they are trying to get out. You need to knock the stone down, sit on it, and set them free.

Some Christians like to erect stones. They enjoy rolling the stone in front of the tomb. Peering at the door of the tomb, they say, "Is he in there? Don't let that joker out, God's gonna get him!" Let me tell you something, God's not trying to "get" anyone. If He were, we'd all be dead by now.

Let go of the status quo mindset of dead religion and realize that you serve a God Who can do the impossible. Start walking in the light of His glory. Realize that Jesus is alive, and the holy angels of God are all across this earth looking to help people who have the guts and tenacity to believe God. Do you know what will happen when you do? Jesus will move the stones holding you in. Quit being distracted by the lies of the enemy and the foolishness of fear—start just believing what the Word of God has to say. His Words minister life to you. They will lift you up and refresh your spirit. God will open your eyes to things you never even recognized before.

Millions of good Christian people are struggling with the feeling of finality in their own individual tombs—they feel helpless, as if a stone has shut them in forever. But Jesus came to set all of us free. He rose so that we can rise up in life and not be bound by the devil and all the problems he tries to kill us with.

We weren't saved just so we can live miserably. We weren't given the victory so we could stay defeated in our heart, our mind, and our life. We weren't made free just to fall in a rut! We've been made free through Jesus to get out of what's holding us back in our heart and in our mind. The stone has been rolled away; now it's time we see our freedom and plant ourselves on that stone that is trying to hold us back.

Satan would try to deceive you, maybe even send well-meaning people to tell you it's only natural that you stay in the tomb. He's a liar and the father of all lies. Satan would try to roll the stone back once you begin walking in freedom—and tell you that you're too weak to stay out of what once held you back. Again, he's a deceiver and a liar.

Don't let the devil convince you of what God *can't* do in your life. He's a defeated foe, but he still roams this earth like a lion, looking for whom he may devour (1 Peter 5:8). He isn't a lion though; he's just roaring like one. Realize that greater is He Who is in you than he that is in the world, and put that problem in its place—under your seated body! It's time to sit on the problem.

You know, this world is getting sicker and more twisted by the minute. Things we once thought were evil are now rubberstamped as natural and even normal. We've normalized stones. I believe we are barreling toward the end of this age and Jesus is coming! Many are falling away from the faith, and the Bible said that would happen. In this world, right is wrong, and we're persecuted for believing in Jesus. This is no time to play games with the devil. It's time to stand up for what we believe—and not just to the outside world, but to *ourselves.*

It's time to grow up, knock those stones down, and sit on them. When people talk about power but produce weakness, I can nearly guarantee that in their everyday thoughts, they are consistently either elevating the stones or ignoring the stones—they may even make excuses for the stones and call them good. It's crazy what people will do to keep their stones in place when they don't want let go, but there is freedom in letting go and moving on.

People who are "more than conquerors" don't look at the size of the stone; they grind the stone to powder and hurl the dust ball back at the forces of evil! That may be a strange example, but in spiritual terms, it's the truth. In Luke 20:18,

Jesus said, *"Whosoever shall fall upon that stone shall be broken; but on whomsoever it shall fall, it will grind him to powder."*

I've learned to grind the devil to powder and blow his dust away. And I've been against some of the biggest stones you've ever seen. The devil has tried to kill me many times. But the Bible says that with long life He will satisfy me (Psalm 91:16), so I don't listen when my mind tries to get me to doubt. I don't put the power of Satan or his angels (or any problem he throws) above the One Who sent that angel to roll the stone away.

As long as there is a sinner in this world, there should be a pulpit. Our testimonies of what God has done in our life are the perfect pulpit to not just share Jesus, but also show what Jesus can do in someone's life. The harvesters are headed our way—time is speeding up and we don't have time to placate our flesh, dabble with the devil, or let go of our belief in the present power of Jesus Christ.

As long as we have breath in our body and as long as the world is still in need of His salvation, we should be sitting on those stones proclaiming that He is risen! Like those women at the tomb so long ago, we should be looking to tell somebody that Jesus is alive, and He's alive in us! So, let that angel at the empty tomb be an inspiration to you, like it was to me. Because your life matters to everyone you interact with—you are a walking testament to God's love, grace, and power, and others need to see it.

Conquer what's holding you back. Roll the stones away from the tombs in your life and act just like that angel sitting on the stone that was rolled away—because you can use every obstacle as a pulpit to proclaim and show that Jesus is alive and victorious in *you.*

CHAPTER 5

STRESS FOR A GOOD CAUSE AND RESTORATIVE, ANGELIC SLEEP

When I was in my thirties, I was in that mode of just working myself crazy. I was preaching almost every day. I was studying the Word and doing administrative things, too. I was running myself ragged by not even sleeping very much. I already don't need as much sleep as some people do. I never have. I've always been able to feel great on between four and six hours of sleep, but I wasn't even getting that. I didn't tell my wife, Cathy, but I was starting to have chest pains every day. The stress of sheer working and not sleeping was having a negative effect on my body, but I refused to pay any attention to that.

Sometimes in the ministry, people can get so focused on the vision God has given them to preach the Gospel that they neglect their own body. I've been guilty of this. It's hard when you know people are dying and going to hell, and that hearing about Jesus and accepting His sacrifice is all they need to do to get right with God. I remember when I was about 35 years old, or maybe a little younger, I was in this mode of living that all I did was preach, preach, and preach. I wasn't thinking at all about my body or if I needed more sleep. I was just running ninety to nothing with the vision on my mind.

Now, I'm very focused on what God has called me to do—I believe in being diligent and working hard, especially when you're trying to help other people know God. But, even a good intention can hurt you if you don't take care of the vessel God gave you for this journey of life. Today, I'm a lot older in the ministry and God has shown me that I don't have to live stressed in order to complete my destiny or reach my destination in Him. In fact, if I do take on stress, He's shown me that I'm not living by faith but living by my own strength—and there is nothing I can do in my own strength that is as good as He can do through me by simply believing and obeying Him.

When I was running myself ragged for a good cause, I did sometimes feel a nudge in my spirit that I should rest more than I was doing. I just didn't listen to that. Sometimes when you are hyper-focused on a vision, you second-guess anything that comes into your mind that would make you slow up on that vision. I knew that it was very important to reach others for God, but what I didn't realize was that I could shorten my life if I didn't consider the body God gave me. That never crossed my mind then.

In those days, I didn't stay in hotels as much as I stayed in guest rooms, either at the pastor's house or on the church property. Many small churches had what they called "evangelist quarters" on the church property, and I stayed in plenty of those. But for this particular meeting, I was staying at the pastor's house and he had a bunch of those little weenie dogs. This was in a small town in central Louisiana.

That night I remember my body was really hurting. I was exhausted, my chest was tight, and I felt something in my body just wasn't right. Even though I needed to sleep, I just wanted to read the Word and get more in me for the meeting. I remember sitting up in bed with my back against the headboard, and even though I could feel my body hurting, I was looking through the scriptures and reading. I always read the Word before bed, even if it's just one verse. I like to put scripture in my mind right before I sleep. This is a habit I've had for as long as I can remember, since I've been saved.

Well, that night, I was way beyond a few scriptures and as I was looking down at my Bible reading, I felt something in the air change and I looked up—and right in front of my eyes was a huge angel. I'm talking over seven feet tall, at least, and maybe even eight or nine, I don't know, but he was huge and he was close to me. He was shining. There was this glow around him. It was like a bright white light in that room.

I never heard him walk or move, but he just was there as if he just materialized or something. This was not a vision from God or a trick of my tired mind. I could physically see this being standing right in front of me. He had long, blond hair. It wasn't white blond, but was more golden, and his head was just huge—bigger than a human being's head. His whole form was bigger. I was shocked. I just froze.

All I could say was, "Whoa!" I know that's dumb, but I'm telling you that when an angel shows up, you just kind of go blank for a second. Now, I wasn't scared. Even though it was night and I was sitting up in bed, and this bright huge being had just popped right into the room, I was strangely calm. But the dogs? Those weenie dogs wouldn't shut up!

Those dogs were going flat nuts. They'd found a way to bust into my room and were acting crazy. I'm convinced they could see the angel too, because they were all shook up. First, they were barking because they were scared. Then, it was like they were just barking to bark, as if they were trying to talk to the angel! They were walking back and forth, moving around in circles like they were nervous, and barking right in his direction. They kept running away and then running back to look at him—and bark.

I could hardly believe my eyes, but that angel turned to those dogs to look at them and touched them, and then he looked right back at me. If they kept barking after that, I don't know because I couldn't hear them. It was like whatever sounds were happening, all of it was just drowned out while I was looking at this massive angel.

That one word, "Whoa," was all I said before the angel said this: "I have been sent by the Lord. You are under much stress, and the Lord sent me to tell you to sleep." I'm serious. That is what he said.

Now, you'd think if an angel shows up, he's going to always tell you something profound or prophetic—but sometimes, I guess, God sends them to protect you even from yourself! They are the Help, and I sure did need some help. I was killing myself with too much work, and I don't know, maybe that was a critical moment for my physical body. I do know now that God had more for me to do, and that night was important enough to Him to send the Help to help me out.

"I have been sent by the Lord. You are under much stress, and the Lord sent me to tell you to sleep," the angel said, and I just accepted what he said as true. It was like he was waiting for that, for me to accept what he said, because once I did? He was just gone. He didn't walk out of the room; he just disappeared into the air.

Now, I know some people don't believe me, but I do not care! When you have an experience like that—or any other angelic experience that is physically right in front of your face—nobody is going to be able to talk you out of it with their judgments or doubts. At some point, when it comes to the things of God that go against natural law, you just come to accept that His ways are just flat higher than your ways, and that what God and His angelic beings are capable of is more than your natural brain can really grasp. There are some things that are just unknowable while we're here on this earth, and that's just the way it is.

When the angel left, the Bible I'd been holding fell perfectly right onto my chest and I immediately fell asleep—and when I woke up, I realized that it wasn't my usual four, five, or six hours on a good night's sleep. I had slept a solid 12 hours! Now, that may not be unusual for some people, but I couldn't remember ever in my whole life sleeping that much. Even as a kid or a teenager, I didn't sleep that much. So, I was shocked when I woke up at 12 noon with that Bible still laying right on my chest in perfect position. I felt like a million bucks!

All the pain in my chest was gone. My mind was at ease. There was a calm over me that felt great. I was rested, I mean fully rested, and it was like my body was relieved and had been restored. It's amazing what a good night's rest can do, but buddy, I'm telling you, it's phenomenal what angelic sleep can do!

I got up quickly and was a little concerned because I'd slept so long at the pastor's house. I thought maybe he and his wife would be worried about me or think badly of me just laying in the bed so long. I knew I was supposed to meet them for breakfast. So, I got up and ran out of the guest room as fast as I could. When I saw the pastor, the first thing he started to do was apologize to me for his dogs.

I interrupted him and told them, "There was an angel of God in the house last night." And all he could say was, "You know, my dogs were going nuts! I didn't know what was going on. I did everything I could to shut them up." That's when I knew the dogs must have started or continued to bark after the angel spoke and sent me into deep sleep. I don't know. All I know is that the pastor told me he heard them, waited to see if they'd stop, and when they didn't, he came into my room and got them. But they still didn't shut up, and every time he'd get them quiet, they'd start up again.

"I didn't hear them barking," I said. "In fact, I didn't hear anything except that angel of the Lord." You know, after that angel made me sleep, those dogs could have been barking right in my ear and it wouldn't have mattered! I'd have never heard it. When that Bible hit my chest, my eyes went shut, and my body started its 12-hour recuperation, dogs or no dogs! Somebody could have blown a trumpet and I wouldn't have heard it.

Well, the pastor was fascinated by an angel being there and we talked about it, but he was most interested in how he looked.

"What did he look like?" he asked me.

"He was a BIG man," I said, and I started to describe his facial features to the pastor, being sure to tell him that this one God sent to me had no wings at all. He was just like a human but bigger, and glowing like a really bright light bulb . . . and panicking the dogs. We laughed because the pastor had been so worried his beautiful little weenie dogs were keeping me up all night. He was just sure I was going to wake up irritated and never want to come back. The pastor told me, "I kept thinking, man, I'm gonna kill them dogs. That man's trying to sleep!!!"

Animals are very sensitive to spiritual things. They instinctively seem to feel when the Hidden Help show up, and sometimes I think they see them, too—and seeing angels scares them just like it can scare us.

I learned a valuable lesson from that short encounter with an angel, and it was about obedience to take care of the body God has given us. We are spirit beings first. We have a soul. We live in a body. God gives us our body. This earthly vessel we live in is worth listening to and protecting. Life is precious. You only have so many moments, so many heartbeats, and so many breaths to take in this human vessel—and you can't forget that it is a wonderfully made thing. The human body is amazing . . . but it has its limits. If you don't respect those limits, you can push yourself too far even doing something good.

Too much stress for a good cause is still stress, and it can hurt you or even kill you. There's a difference between pushing yourself and going over the limit of what your body can do without damage. God has called us to run our race well, and part of that is knowing that we must pace ourselves to get the best results in our life.

Just like there is a season for everything, there is a time to sprint, a time to go at a steady pace, a time to rest, and a time to go full throttle toward your goal or vision. Nobody can go full throttle 100% of the time, day in and day out, and last long. In fact, the older I get, the more God is using me, and yet the less stress I have while doing it. I'm kind of amazed by that. You'd think that you need to push, push, push internally all the time—but that's not true.

You don't have to stress out all the time to be capable and run with your vision. You don't have to hurt yourself on no sleep to fulfill your destiny or reach your destination. That internal stress that pushes you too much isn't good for your body or your mind. In fact, it's really just taking the cares of it all onto your own back—something God didn't create you to do.

Fear will make you stress out. And the devil can convince you that it's a good thing to stress out for a good cause. You know he comes to steal, kill, and destroy, right? Jesus warned us of this (John 10:10). So, don't think he'll always try to discourage you from your mission or vision, or try to pull you off course—sometimes he'll push you. He'll push, and push, and push you. Because the sooner you're hurt, the better it is for him. The weaker he can get you, the better it is for him. Don't fall for it, even if what you're doing is for a good cause.

Realize that Jesus came to give you life, and life more abundantly . . . faith in God can help you do more with less stress. Faith is amazing like that! Life, and life more abundantly, doesn't mean running through your days like a chicken with its head cut off. It doesn't mean wasting your mental space fretting and worrying. That is no good!

Listen to your body. The signals it sends you are there for your own good. If it tells you to rest, then rest. It'll warn you when you push it beyond the limits of what it can do without being damaged. Just like God had more for me to do and a lesson I needed to learn, I believe that God has more for you to do . . . and lessons you need to learn, too.

Angels are always around, whether we see them or not. This natural world is so much smaller than the spiritual world. God has a plan for each of our lives individually that we can see fulfilled when we follow Him. We must realize that even if we live to 120 years, that's still a drop in the bucket compared to eternity. By sending that angel, God showed me that I only have so much time to do what I need to do here on earth. And in order to fulfill His plan for me, I cannot ignore the body He gave me—even for the greatest cause in the world.

I hope this story helps you to see the same thing. You've got more to do. You've got more to say. You've got more people to bless and influence to go in the right direction—God's direction. Rest up for it!

CHAPTER 6

Angelic Experiences Don't Build More Faith in God

Whenever I share an angelic experience, there is always somebody who tells me, "Oh, I wish I'd see what you've seen!" or "Why haven't I ever seen something like that from God?" That's a question I can't answer. I do know that a lot of people I've talked to think that if they just saw something like I've seen, they'd have greater faith. I mean, you'd think if someone saw an angel of God or even been rescued from some kind of catastrophe, they'd believe and follow God, right?

All we have to do to dispel that lie is read the Word. Faith comes by hearing, and hearing the Word of God (Romans 10:17). It doesn't come by seeing angels. But what if someone saw the Son of God walking around and healing people? You'd think they'd believe if they saw Jesus doing miracles, right? The Word throws that lie right out the window, too.

There were people who saw the miracles of Jesus who didn't believe—some even said demons helped Him work miracles

(Matthew 12:24). There were others who saw Him do miracles and praised Him for those miraculous works, and still they betrayed Him in life. Remember that many of the same people who praised Jesus into town with palm leaves waving ended up turning on Him and crying out, "Crucify Him!" not too much later (Matthew 21:6-9; 27:22-23). If that's not proof that people are fickle and don't gain faith by witnessing supernatural things, I don't know what is.

Words are what God used to form this world. The Bible says that Heaven and Earth will pass away, but His Word will never pass away. Hearing is not just about sound waves going into our ears, but about what we allow to sink down deep into our heart—the more of God's Word we hear, the more our faith builds. That's how God made us.

Jesus was God in the flesh, coming down to rescue His creation from the sin-sick state of being that had permeated the whole world after the fall of man. Jesus' words were so truthful that they cut through human hypocrisy like a sword. People didn't like that back then. They don't like it today. People like what's comfortable and easy to hear.

People like the miracles, but they don't always like truth—and even if God parted the sea for them, they might still choose not to believe. That happened before Jesus ever came on the scene, back when Moses led the Israelite slaves out of Egypt. Those people saw all the plagues and the supernatural events that led to their freedom from bondage. They even walked through a parted Red Sea when Pharaoh changed his mind and sent an army to capture them and bring them back into slavery.

Yet it's not that long before many of those freed slaves, who saw God do the supernatural, gave up on Him and started worshiping false gods—and that's because seeing and experiencing do *not* guarantee believing. It's not automatic.

Think about it. While Moses is literally up the mountain getting the Ten Commandments written by the finger of God Himself, those fools were down in the valley making golden idols of cows and thinking it was alright (Exodus 32:7-8,19-24).

The bottom line: you'll never get more faith in God by seeing angels or any sign or wonder. Those things can only support your faith, but they can't produce it. So, again, because I really want you to get this: the only way you create faith in your heart for God is by *"hearing, and hearing by the Word of God."* Faith doesn't come by seeing and seeing; it comes by hearing and hearing. Seeing can astound you. It can fill your mind with wonder. It can even help to set your life in a new direction where you want to know more about God and His truth. But it doesn't produce faith. In fact, Jesus Himself said it's better if you believe and *don't* see (John 20:29). That means you can have faith and see things, but the ones who don't see and yet believe are in a better position to God in Heaven. Glory!

Some people in this world seem just more prone to seeing into the spirit world. They have a gift of some sort, but just because a person is gifted doesn't mean they are using that gift in truth or with a right spirit. The Word says the gifts of God are *without* repentance—and that means even the unsaved and deceived may have spiritual sightings that believers don't have. Their gift is not dependent on their faith. It's a gift God created, but they could easily reject the truth for a lie and use their gift to support the lies of the devil.

Who knows why some are given the gift of sight in that area? That's God's business, not ours. We each have gifts that are given to us that God gave to us for a reason—and He wants us to use what He's given us in our individual lives. Envying somebody else's gift just sets you up for inner strife and takes away your recognition and appreciation for the wonderful gifts God has given you.

Some people hear my experiences and tell me they remember times in their lives that they wished an angel had intervened—hearing any experience where God intervened makes them angry and bitter. This is tough because while we all want smooth sailing with no loss or trouble in life, bitterness and resentment don't bring any relief to the human heart. They don't help anyone release hurt or heal. And while I don't know why The Hidden Help intervene in certain situations and not others, I believe that God knows something we don't—and the best thing we can do is remember that God loves us and is with us, but there is an enemy on the earth that only comes to steal, kill, and destroy (John 10:10).

God knows what we don't. God's thoughts are higher than our thoughts and so are His ways (Isaiah 55:8-9). He knows why certain moments matter in the scheme of things and why angels must intervene—and we are not God's judge. So, all the "whys" that involve judging God when it comes to past events we wish had turned out differently are fruitless mind games that bring no peace.

The Word tells us that the secret things belong to the Lord (Deuteronomy 29:29). He may or may not choose to reveal the whys, but if we want to be free in our own heart and not let the past hinder our present and our future, we must trust Him. We must trust that He created us eternal beings and that this world is temporary, along with all of its hurts and pain. He has promised that He is near to the broken hearted and that no matter what has happened, we have the victory over the devil and all his works through Jesus Christ.

Trusting in the Lord and His Word, that's what real faith in God is all about. We don't have to know all the whys to trust God and continue in our faith. With or without the obvious intervention of the Hidden Help, we can be sure that God sees it all, and because of His saving love, we can find peace no matter what has happened in this temporal life. His Word reminds us that while we live in a spiritual war, His plans aren't for our harm—His plans for us are for good and not evil, and He *always* has our best interests at heart (Jeremiah 29:11).

There are many angels helping and ministering to us from the spirit world, but there are also many fallen angels who live in that realm too, and are doing their best to steal, kill, and destroy God's people in this world. There are many types and varieties of angels, but the most important distinction you can make is just between the two groups—the ones who serve God and want to help and the ones who serve Satan and want to harm. That's it. God told us to choose which we will serve. We shouldn't ever fall into the trap of blaming God for what the devil and his demons do—but don't you worry; their day is coming!

Hell was created for the devil and all the fallen angels, and one day you will see them all kicked into the lake of fire as an eternal punishment for every single thing they did. From turning their backs on a good God to hurting what He loves—you and me, and all of the creation we see around us that He meant for us to enjoy. Satan and the fallen angels will experience the wrath and final judgement of God Almighty.

So, if you've lost a battle, the war isn't over. Jesus is coming back, just like He said He would. Don't listen to the scoffers, the ones who leave the faith or water down the truth of God's Word. The Bible warns us that there will be a great falling away before Jesus comes, among a lot of other things, of course. But I want you to remember that the Word tells us people will leave the faith in droves before Jesus comes back—they will mock believers who say Jesus is coming and say, "They've been saying that forever!" Sounds like what's going on today, doesn't it?

I don't know about you, but I'm never leaving my faith behind. What could I possibly want to go back to? What in Hell do I want? Nothing! God has everything good in store for me, and I'm not giving up for that loser, Satan, or the angels he convinced way back when to rebel against God. They have caused so much trouble, and they will keep doing it until the end.

So, I go about my days in joy and with a good heart no matter what they are doing. How can I do that? Because Jesus won at the cross, and I'm walking every day in His victory. I enforce Satan's defeat every time I speak the Word, every time I don't bend to the pressures of the world, and every time I receive what God has for me. Glory!

Satan fights people because he hates God, and because God loves people. So, over my many years of serving the Lord, I've learned to rise above his attacks—I live free and let the Word of God fight for me. I put it in my heart and it comes out of my mouth in faith, and it cuts the devil's plans to shreds.

Faith is peaceful. When you *know* that you know . . . well, you *know!* So, I refuse to live in fear and worry. I live free in Jesus. I'm joyful because that's a fruit of God's Spirit and I choose to walk in it. Every day is a choice to put God first and believe what He said in His Word. Every day is an opportunity to let Christ live through me.

I've adopted for my own life what Paul said in Galatians 2:20: "*I have been crucified with Christ; it is no longer I who live, but Christ lives in me; and the life which I now live in the flesh I live by faith in the Son of God, Who loved me and gave Himself for me*" (NKJV). This is a self-centered world because the ruler of it is Satan, and he self-authored pride and doing things his way. But as a believer, I reject living his way and my aim is to live Christ-centered every day. That means putting God first, living by childlike faith in His Word, acting on my faith, and being amazed at what happens.

How can I live this way in a sin-sick world run amok? Because I know that I'm going to live forever and that all this is temporary—Jesus is coming! Either He comes to me or I go to Him, but either way, Heaven awaits. So, I decided to take the Lord's prayer to heart and start practicing. I want His will to be done on earth as it is in Heaven (Matthew 6:9-10). Is it His will for me to be sad, sick, and disgusted? No. Is it His will for me to live in fear and worry, wringing my hands about what the devil is doing? No. I preach the Gospel because I love Jesus and because He said in Mark 16:15 to *"Go ye into all the world, and preach the Gospel to every creature"*—that's my part.

I wasn't always this way. If you know my testimony, you know that I was a rock musician who didn't care about God at all. I wasn't an atheist; I was just completely indifferent and focused only on myself. After I got saved, I had a lot to learn . . . I mean, a lot! After nearly 50 years of knowing the Lord, I'd say I've learned a lot about how to live for God.

I'm not perfect, far from it. But I'm much better than when I started out—my wife, Cathy, says it's like night and day! I went to my 50th class reunion and they voted me "Most Changed." It made me laugh because if you knew me before, you wouldn't have ever believed I'd be a preacher of the Gospel. But that's the power of Jesus. That's the power of salvation.

Every day with the Lord, even after all these years, I learn more, share more, and get better at using my faith. Spiritually, physically, and financially, I know that God is concerned about every part of my life—and if I put Him first and just do what He said, I know that even His angels will get involved in bringing His Word to pass in my life. It's amazing!

You see, I know there's a war going on between God and the enemy, but I'm on the right side of the war—God's side. And because I've read the back of the Book, I know that no matter what Satan does, we win! When it's all said and done, we WIN! We don't just win once . . . we win *forever*. And it's all because of Jesus: the One Who went out of His way to reach me.

CHAPTER 7

Wanting to Give Up and Going to Don and Curley's

Let me tell you a little story from long ago when I first got saved. If you know anything about me, you know that I love preaching and seeing people lifted out of the clutches of sin and the life-destroying tactics of the devil. One reason I love it so much is because that's exactly what God did for me. He totally changed my life. But in the first year of my salvation, I almost backslid and went right back to my old ways. Satan knows how to get people in their weak spots, and back then, my biggest weak spot was my temper.

I had a hot head. I used to blame it on my Cajun heritage. "I've got Tabasco sauce running through my veins!" I'd say. You see, I was the kind of man that could go from irritation to full blown anger in just a few minutes. Some said that I had an anger problem. My response to that was, "I don't have a problem. But if you make me angry, it's *you* that's gonna have a problem! Leap, frog!"

At the time, there was a show called "The Incredible Hulk" on television, and whenever the heat started rising in my veins, my wife would see it and crack a joke. She and my daughter would say, "He's turning green! Look, he's turning green!" That would make me laugh and diffuse it enough to help me calm down. Still, I walked around with my fuse ready to be lit at a moment's notice.

Now, many people assume that salvation immediately changes your weaknesses. They think the moment you say the Lord's prayer, you suddenly get a new personality. It's not true. You get a new, recreated spirit, but your soul—which is your mind, will, and emotions—well, those change in time as you renew your mind to the Word of God. The less you are *conformed to this world*" and the more you apply the Word you read, the more you are *"transformed by the renewing of your mind"* (Romans 12:2). That's a process and it doesn't happen overnight, which brings me to this story of when God sent an angel to help me out.

I'd been saved less than a year and I had decided to throw in the towel. I was what people called a "baby Christian," and I had my soulish Pampers diapers on tight. I had a lot of joy over what God had done for me, but all it took was a slap to knock that right out of me. Now, I have to say this too. Before I came to know the Lord through a Billy Graham crusade on television, I was a rock entertainer and I drank a lot. I started my day with a bottle of whiskey and that was way before my "fun" drinking started. I liked drugs, too. You could say I took trips and never left my house. So, when God came into my life and all that stopped in an instant, it blew my wife away. It amazed me, too, that the desire just left me. I was truly a new man and stopped cold turkey without any thought about it. Everybody who knew me could hardly believe it.

That day I was witnessing for Jesus, and my whole heart was into telling this person about God. I had so much joy that if you had told me that only a few hours later I was about to leave my new life in Christ behind and go back to my old ways, I never would have believed you.

You see, I had been talking with this man and he and I were going back and forth. At some point he got flat angry at me for telling Him what was right in God's sight, and he just stopped talking and slapped me right in the face. I was shocked at first, and then I got HOT. Tabasco hot! The anger rose in me so fast that I knew I had to get out or I was going to lose it. I knew that I was supposed to "turn the other cheek," and so I went against my hot-headed nature and I did it.

Turning the other cheek is easier said than done . . . even if you do it! I learned that the minute I got into my car to drive home, because with every second in that car alone, I just kept getting madder than hell. You see, a slap is hard for a man like me to take. I'm from another generation than today. If somebody throws a punch, that's not as hard to take mentally because at least it's manly. But a slap? A slap is totally disrespectful! Before I was saved, if you slapped me, I'd be looking for a pipe or something to hit you—because the payback for a slap *has* to be much worse.

As I drove, what was bothering more than anything was that God didn't stop it from happening. I couldn't take it. I couldn't believe that God would let somebody slap me for talking about Him. It shows how immature in the faith I really was. I mean, I honestly thought that if I was on the right track and doing good things for God, He'd make sure nothing bad happened. Sure, I knew that whoever I was witnessing to might not accept Jesus when I shared my faith, but it never crossed my mind that God would let them raise a hand to me.

Man, was I totally misguided! The Word is *full* of stories of God's people being persecuted for His name's sake. It's funny to me now when I think about how indignant I got over being slapped when, throughout biblical history, God's people have been boiled in oil, hung upside down on crosses, and stoned to death! Still, back then, I didn't think about all of that. I was just plain mad!

So, what did I do? I rehearsed how it happened in my mind over and over as I drove. I started talking to God aloud, just hollering in my car and spitting fire. I got home and told Cathy, and that just made it worse—it was like the more I told her how I felt, the angrier and angrier I got. Something snapped in me, and I decided right then and there that I was DONE with everything.

I told Cathy I was not going to live some life where God doesn't step in when somebody tries to hit me, and that was that. At that moment, I realized all I really wanted was a drink, so I said it, "I'm done with this God junk! I'm going to get drunk!" I told Cathy I was going to Don and Curley's Bar, which was this place downtown. Now, my wife got *upset*. Cathy is not an overly emotional or dramatic woman—but she was flat upset. She begged me not to go, but I couldn't be stopped. I was too mad. I didn't want to hear a word she had to say about God or anything. I was going to get drunk as a skunk, and that was that.

Cathy told me later that she started praying in the Holy Spirit the minute I left the house. If I'd have seen her pray, I wouldn't have cared anyway. I've always been the kind of man who couldn't be deterred if I made up my mind about something.

So, I was driving to Don and Curley's Bar and cussing up a storm in my car on the way. Cathy later told me that during that time, she was praying hard. She said that all she could think of was how I'd had such a beautiful deliverance from alcohol—that God had saved me from so much—and that she didn't want to see me fall back into that lifestyle and leave God's path for my life. So, she prayed hard in the Holy Spirit. And in the middle of that praying, Cathy would later tell me that she felt some wisdom and insight come into her mind. She said that she knew she needed to "plead the blood" of Jesus over me, and so that's what she did.

While I was driving and angry, leaving my faith behind, Cathy was at the house speaking my name and pleading the blood of Jesus over me. She was walking around that house as she prayed, acting out the Old Testament story of when the children of Israel put blood on the doorposts so the angel of death would avoid their houses during the plagues against Egypt. She was saying, "I plead the blood of Jesus over Jesse! Lord, protect Him . . ." and other things like that as she walked through our little house, figuratively painting the blood of Jesus over all the doors as she called my name out to the Lord. Her whole heart was spiritually focused in my direction.

I pulled up to Don and Curley's and parked the car. When I tried to open the door, it wouldn't open. It would *not* open. At first, I thought the door was just stuck. It'd never been stuck before, but I figured something had happened and it was stuck. So, I pulled the lever to open the door and jammed it with my shoulder to try and get it to budge. It wouldn't budge. I kept pulling the lever over and over. I kept pushing at the door. That's when I started hollering at God about everything that happened. I was talking to Him, to myself, and to the door and I was cussing at all three. The car was fine and I'd never had a problem with the door before. I can't even describe to you how hot under the collar I got in that car. All I wanted to do was get in that bar and something wouldn't let me.

Baam! Baam! Baam! I'd hit that door over and over, and it wouldn't budge. I was doing everything I knew to do. I thought about busting the glass, but I didn't want to have to pay the bill to replace it. *Baam! Baam! Baam!* I just kept hitting it. I told myself that once I got out of that blankety-blank-blank car I was going to tell everybody I knew to forget about all this God junk.

Then, all of a sudden, in the middle of that rage, I yelled out, "God! He slapped me! I was talking about You and he slapped me!" I felt something come over me and I heard in my spirit: "They slapped Me, too. They spit on Me. They pulled out My beard." I froze in that car for a moment. The words just stopped me in my tracks.

All of a sudden, the anger subsided and I just felt convicted. I didn't feel bad for what I was doing. I didn't feel any guilt. It was more like I just suddenly saw what I was doing. Like I suddenly grasped what I was really doing and the decision I was making to really leave God . . . all because of a slap while I was witnessing.

They slapped Jesus . . . they spit on Him and pulled out His beard. How weak am I? How dumb? I thought. And I remember saying aloud to myself, "If I can't handle this one little lick . . ." and then I started laughing at myself. "Boy, I'm about the weakest Christian I guess anybody could ever be!" I said to myself in that car.

In the Cajun culture of my youth, we used to use a phrase called a "no-count weak puppy" to describe somebody that can't do anything for themselves, and that's what I saw myself as right then. Sitting in front of Don and Curley's with a door that just would not open for anything, I felt the weight of making the decision to leave God and tell everybody about it, and then wanting to get drunk on top of it too—I humbled myself before God. Inside that car, with the door that wouldn't open, I said, "Lord, forgive me." My hand was still on the door lever when I asked for forgiveness, and the strangest thing happened just then. *Chi-chick.* The lever opened the door. I couldn't believe it.

Now, I had been banging on that door. I'd been pushing on that door. My hand had been on the lever the whole time. And I couldn't get out of the car. Well, I couldn't get out until I said those words, until my heart shifted—because before, when I was about to run headlong into sin, there was something barring the door. But after saying "forgive me," it opened like it always did before. I looked at that door and closed it. I opened the door, looked at that bar I was sitting in front of, and closed the door again. I opened and closed the door over and over, just to check the lever and the locks.

There was no problem with the door. Cathy likes to say that it's because she was pleading the blood of Jesus over every door at our house during this time—that she was praying for me and for my protection. Do you know what? I believe her. There was something holding that door and keeping me from opening it, and I believe it was the Hidden Help I didn't want. But Cathy did want that help. She's connected to me. She's my wife and my best friend. She loves me more than any other person on this planet, and that day she loved me enough to send the Hidden Help.

God hears the earnest prayers of the righteous. The energy of prayer is powerful and draws on the power of the Lord. To this day, I know that an angel of God was holding that door. I mean, I hit it so hard with my shoulder that I actually bruised it trying to open it. I had a bruise for a week to remind me. There was nothing wrong with those locks. I had that car for years and never had a problem with the door before or after that day. That was an intervention. That was the Hidden Help.

When I got home, I walked through the front door and there was Cathy with eyes as big as saucers. "Did ya . . . did ya go drinking?" she asked. I said, "No." It took me a second, but then I decided just to tell her, "I couldn't get out of that car. I tried to open up that car . . ." and she said, "The angel of God was holding his hand on that door because I was praying, and I pled the blood." I said, "You pled the what?" She said, "I pled the blood! Boy, I had the blood all over you! I was not gonna let you go back into that stuff."

I often wonder why the Hidden Help intervenes sometimes and not others. I can't tell you why God's servants stop some things and let others happen. I don't know what would have happened or how my life would have changed had I been able to open that door and go into that bar. What would have happened if I'd just gone in, talked bad about God and Christianity, and just started drinking myself back into my old life.

I do know that if I had really left God, I sure wouldn't have ever become a preacher—and so everything that I've done to witness for God from that day until now wouldn't have happened. There's a good chance I would have drunk myself to death because before I got saved, I drank so much a doctor once told me I'd be dead of cirrhosis of the liver in my twenties if I didn't stop. At that time, I was newly born again and just had a regular job. I didn't have any thoughts about being a minister. That was as far from my mind as possible. Apparently, it wasn't that far from God's mind, though—He knows the future. I believe that day in front of Don and Curley's was a pivotal moment for me.

This story is not really about a car door that wouldn't open. It's about God using the Hidden Help at pivotal moments in life. He did it in people's lives in biblical times; He still does it in lives today. That was a pivotal moment in my life. I'd just gotten saved, God had a plan for me, and He sent an angel to make me pause. Sometimes that's all you need when you're taken by your emotions and about to go headlong into something you don't need in your life. We do dumb things when we're angry. Yet God told us it was ok to be angry—just sin not (Ephesians 4:26). Anger isn't a sin. It's what you say and do in that anger that can be sinful.

This is also a story about the power of passionate prayer. You know, Cathy's words to me when I was complaining were loving. She was so concerned, but they weren't enough to stop me. In fact, they angered me more and that's because I didn't want to calm down. I didn't want the kindness. I wanted somebody to get angry with me! So it didn't matter what she said, but what *did* matter is what she did once I left. Cathy prayed in the way the Holy Spirit led her to pray, and it was fervent (James 5:16). She was serious; she did not want me to go back to the life God had just saved me from.

Cathy didn't just throw up her hands and say, "Oh well, I guess that's it." No, she prayed in the Holy Spirit. She prayed hard and her faith was in it. Those weren't just words she was splattering around; her prayer was raw and real, and coming from a place of faith that God would turn my heart, something, anything, to stop me from going off course—and that prayer caught the attention of an angel.

You know, people are always praying for God to open doors for them in life, but I guess that day Cathy was praying the opposite. Sometimes a closed door is the right thing. Sometimes there are places you just don't need to be. Some of those places might not take you off course, but, then again, some might— you really do not know the future or how exactly each choice you make affects your future. But God does. I really believe that had the door not been shut to me, I would have gone another way in life. There was something important about that moment. It was a crossroads.

Only God knows the pivotal moments. And, sometimes, as Cathy says, the most powerful thing you can do is pray when you see somebody going headlong into destruction. Getting into worry or fear won't help anybody. Running after somebody won't always help either. Telling them everything you know is true won't do it either! Sometimes, the only thing that is going to change a situation is pure, strong, from-your-heart prayer. Cathy said I left looking one way and came back looking another way—that I walked through our door like nothing had happened . . . and with a bag of groceries!

I can't really remember any details about going to the grocery store, but I do remember that closed door and I do remember the click that came after I asked for forgiveness. At that point I could have gone into the bar anyway. I could have opened the door and, even with all that, gone in and slid back into my old life . . . because I still had free will. What God gave me with the closed door was a moment to realize that I was totally wrong.

I believe in guardian angels, and that day I believe that Cathy encouraged mine to not just watch me make the wrong choice with my free will, but to put a barrier in place so it would take me a little longer to choose. Hidden Help isn't always an open door; sometimes it's one that's closed so tight you bruise yourself trying to choose badly.

Nobody likes being persecuted for Christ. Nobody likes being hit when they're trying to give someone the gift of Jesus. But, after that incident, I made up my mind that nobody is going to stop me from loving the Lord. Nobody is going to make me so mad that I turn on God. Nobody is going to make me walk away from my salvation. I think I had an angel there that day in the car to help me. And you know, now that I'm older, sometimes I wonder how many times over the years angels have helped me?

Have you ever wondered how many times have they stopped an accident from happening? How many times has God had them sovereignly step in? What moments would have derailed your entire future if you'd gone this way or that? I really do believe that when I pass into Heaven, God is going to roll back the tape, so to speak, and I'm going to get to see just how many times the Lord sent His angelic servants to help me. I believe the same will happen for you. And I believe that those who have prayed in earnest, like Cathy, are going to see the effect those prayers had in the spiritual realm—and how the Hidden Help of angels moved with the Word of God being spoken in faith.

Angels have a different perspective than we do. They see both sides—the physical world we see and the spiritual world we don't. They see the spiritual warfare up close and personal. All the demonic forces, the fallen principalities and powers of the air that work against God's kids, are on full display for God's angels and all the supernatural beings He created. They have no doubt about the duality we live in at all, and they know without any doubt that we have a tempter. It's the same tempter they had, too—Satan and all the ones that fell along with him so long ago. They can't make us do anything, but they can war against the good around us and try to tempt us to go in the way of our unrepentant flesh.

The angels of God know that we are living spiritually blind. The angels of God know the war going on for our very souls. They know we must rely on faith in God to "see"—to have the eyes of our heart opened so that we comprehend the reality going on not only outside in the world, but inside of ourselves.

The prayers of the faithful matter because they move things in the spiritual realm. They are an energetic force that draws attention on the other side—the veiled side where the Hidden Help are watching. So, don't be afraid to pray with your whole heart and all the faith you've got. Remember that, sometimes, people around you may need just that!

You may not know until you cross over into that divine place called Heaven how your prayers here on earth sent angels on assignment. One day, I believe you will see how every *"effectual fervent prayer of the righteous"* lit up the spirit world, drew the attention of God and His angelic host, and created a way for someone—one that never would have happened if you hadn't stepped up to the plate to pray.

CHAPTER 8

THE UNSUNG POWER AND PROTECTION OF "REGULAR" AND GUARDIAN ANGELS

So, let's talk about some of these angels God made! Who are these angels helping us? When it comes to the angelic realm, everybody seems to be fascinated by the seraphim or the cherubim, the archangels, etc., and, I promise, I'll get to those in a second . . . but I just have to first talk about the ones everybody calls "regular" angels. Regular. That's pretty funny because an angel of God is nothing close to being regular. They aren't less than; there are just more of them and they're more active with human beings.

I've seen firsthand in my heavenly experiences that when we pray, the angels who are with us also pray. When we reverence God, they do it along with us. When we praise, angels praise God with us, too. God's wonderful angels rejoice *with* us—they take every opportunity to honor God.

In Genesis 28:12 (NKJV), God gave Jacob a divine dream, and it was a peek into angelic reality: *"Then he dreamed, and behold, a ladder was set up on the earth, and its top reached to Heaven; and there the angels of God were ascending and descending on it."* Invisible. Powerful. Coming and going all the time so that earth is never without them, the dream God gave Jacob lets us know that there's always a fresh set of angels coming!

The spiritual reality is that if you're saved, *you've* been ministered to by angels. How can I say that? Because the Word says it! Hebrews 1:14 (NKJV) says, *"Are they not all ministering spirits sent forth to minister for those who will inherit salvation?"* The ministering spirits that were at work in Jesus' ministry are still here today—they have never stopped ministering!

The Psalmist David even sung to them, saying, *"Bless the Lord, ye His angels, that excel in strength, that do His commandments, hearkening unto the voice of His word. Bless ye the Lord, all ye His hosts; ye ministers of His, that do His pleasure"* (Psalm 103:20-21). In the very next chapter, he sings about God, saying that He is the One *"Who makes His angels spirits, His ministers a flame of fire"* (Psalm 104:4 NKJV).

After Satan tempted Jesus in the wilderness, the Word says, *"Then the devil leaveth Him, and, behold, angels came and ministered unto Him"* (Matthew 4:11). They'd seen the whole temptation of Jesus up close and personal, and they were right there after Satan fled, ready to be there for Jesus—because that's one of the many things God's angels do. The affect these "regular" angels have is greater than any of us realize—they assist the Holy Spirit right here on earth to draw the lost, and they help believers in times of need, too. And, if you never feel or see one, let me tell you something, you have still experienced them. That's right. That's what Hebrews 1:14 is saying. Isn't that amazing?

As I said earlier, we don't know all the things *any* of the angelic beings do, including the "regular" angels. But if you read through the Word and see how many times they were involved in events, volumes could be written on their service to God.

Now I want to share a little bit on what people call "guardian angels," because I believe many of the angels here have this duty. I know that some people don't believe in guardian angels, but I do. Some people think this is a bunch of hogwash for kids. Maybe they've seen too much old religious children's art or seen too many movies! Look at what the Word says: *"For He shall give His angels charge over thee, to keep thee in all thy ways. They shall bear thee up in their hands, lest thou dash thy foot against a stone"* (Psalm 91:11-12). Notice it's plural. That means the old idea that you have just one angel is what's hogwash!

All of Psalm 91 is about the safety of *abiding* in the presence of God, and verses eleven and twelve tell us that, when we do, God's angels are in charge of watching out for our safety. They have a responsibility for us. That passage is where we get our understanding of angels who guard God's people.

To understand how this guardianship works, you've got to put Psalm 91:12 in context. Most people don't do that, and so they totally misunderstand. They read that scripture and think that angels should save them no matter what. That's totally false. Remember that the devil tried this deceptive idea with Jesus during the three temptations in Matthew 4:6. He quoted the guardian angel scripture and told Jesus to throw Himself off a cliff, since God said He'd send angels to save Him. Jesus shut that fool down in a hurry because He knew Satan was twisting what God said. Jesus refused and just quoted the Word: *"Thou shalt not tempt the Lord thy God"* (Matthew 4:7).

You see, angels are under no obligation to save you from doing dumb things, like throwing yourself off a cliff to test and see if angels will come, like the devil suggested Jesus do. In fact, they are under no obligation to save you at all if you aren't doing what Psalm 91 says to do—because there is a clear *condition* to meet for God to give His angels charge over you.

What is the condition for guardianship? It's the first verse of Psalm 91: *"He who dwells in the secret place of the Most High shall abide under the shadow of the Almighty"* (NKJV). If you meet that condition, the Word promises this: *"Because you have made the Lord Who is my refuge, Even the Most High, your dwelling place, No evil shall befall you, Nor shall any plague come near your dwelling. For He shall give His angels charge over you, To keep you in all your ways. In their hands they shall bear you up, Lest you dash your foot against a stone"* (Psalm 91:9-12 NKJV).

Dwelling or abiding in Him is the key, knowing that He is your refuge—your trusted Shelter from whatever seeks to inflict evil or harm on your body. Jesus took it further when He said, *"If you abide in Me, and My words abide in you, you will ask what you desire, and it shall be done for you. By this My Father is glorified, that you bear much fruit; so you will be My disciples"* (John 15:7-8 NKJV). So, not only are you protected when you abide, but when you abide in Jesus and His Words abide in you, you can ask for what your heart desires.

The word *abide* in the scripture is the same word we use for *stay*, as in where you're staying—it means you're stable and fixed. It's the same word that was used when the disciples asked Jesus where He was staying, so it can also refer to a dwelling place. Think about that and then read that condition again in Psalm 91:1—it's about making the Lord your home, your dwelling, and the place you go to rest and find refuge from whatever else is outside of Him.

When you go to God in prayer, when you fellowship with Him throughout your day, do you feel like you're *home*? Is He your dwelling place, and do you abide (stay) there? These verses challenge us to realize that God must be our dwelling place, because that's how we get under His protective shadow. And who carries out a lot of those protective interventions as we go about our day? The answer is, His servants: the guardian angels who are stationed here to enforce the Word along with us, to help us on our path through this life.

A lot of people think of abiding as being so heavenly minded that you're of no earthly good—that it means you have to walk around like a monk, always being serious and never having fun. That is so far from reality, it's not even funny. People ask me how long I pray, and I always say, "I don't always pray long, but I never go long without praying." You see, prayer is about fellowship to me. Prayer is communication. It's relationship. It's talking to God and listening to Him, and I do that all throughout my day.

I do pray in the Holy Spirit and intercede for people and situations. I have times when I shut the door, so to speak, and have that longer prayer time. But, mostly, I just never go long without praying. You see, I enjoy my relationship with the Lord. I love talking to Him, and I love listening to Him, too. I don't consider prayer something I just do and then get up and go about my day without any more interaction with the Lord. No indeed!

I enjoy my life being under God's shadow. I can't tell you how many times He's saved me from destructive plans the enemy may have had for me, because the only instances I know of were the obvious close calls. But I know that the Hidden Help work on my behalf, and it's the situations I don't know about—the plans I didn't realize that were meant to harm me that they anonymously and secretly saved me from—that I'll find out about when I get to Heaven. That's what the "regular" angels that guard us do, and it's a blessing!

Jesus said that His sheep know His voice and a stranger they will not follow (John 10:4-5). After we get saved, we start learning to tune into His voice—to hear Him—and that comes easiest with daily reading of the Word. The voice of God is present in His Word. It's in His Word where we learn His ways and His will for us.

I think one of the biggest mistakes believers make when they pray (talk to God) is falling into the bad habit of blabbing away, and then getting up and going on their way—forgetting the Lord throughout their day. That's a shallow, one-sided relationship. If you had a friend who did that to you, you'd probably wonder why they didn't want to hear what *you* had to say. Don't do that to the Lord. Cultivate a good relationship. When you pray, be still and welcome His Spirit to speak to your heart. Don't be in a rush to just list out what you need and then be on your way. The Lord wants to be your home place, your dwelling place, and when you abide in Him, you enter into more than just a wonderful relationship; you also set yourself up for the angels to help you, too.

You see, the Word promises that His angels will protect us in direct correlation with how much we dwell in His presence. Religion isn't dwelling in the presence of God. Watching one video a week online to get your church in isn't dwelling in the presence of God. Never talking to God throughout your day isn't dwelling in the presence of God. Remember, God created us to have a relationship with us—we aren't His pets; we're His children. This is about relationship!

Guardian angels serve God's Word and His will—that's Who they are loyal to. If you do what God's Word says, you get what God's Word promises. Sure, the devil may fight you because that's part of life in a fallen world, but he won't win. Because when you have the Word in your heart and it's coming out of your mouth, he's coming up against God and the angels that didn't fall along with him when he tempted them to rebel. He's coming against a Force greater than himself. That

Word you put in your heart is filled with the energy of God Himself because God is one with His Word. John 1:1 says, "*In the beginning was the Word, and the Word was with God, and the Word was God.*" Think about that!

When we dwell in God's presence, we are insulated from all sorts of things. The more Word we have in our heart, the more it comes out of our mouth when the devil fights us—and that activates the angels that work in the invisible spirit world. Because the more we make God our "refuge" and "dwelling place," the more we activate the protective, defensive, safeguarding benefits of the Hidden Help. We must *walk* in the Spirit in order to *receive* from the Spirit.

We do best when we understand the duality of the life we are living—partly in the everyday natural world and partly in the spirit. We live in both when we acknowledge the Spirit of God in our heart throughout the day, when we go about our day enjoying life, working, or doing whatever it is we get to do—but abiding in the Lord through it all. Talk to God throughout your day. Pray and enjoy that prayer. Times in your car, times when you are alone. You don't even have to speak aloud. You can talk to God from your inner man—I do that all the time. It's just part of my life, part of how I dwell in Him and how He dwells in me. Glory!

In John 17, Jesus prays for Himself, His disciples, and all believers. It is fitting here to see Jesus confirm our origin when He tells the Father, "*I have given them Your word; and the world has hated them because they are not of the world, just as I am not of the world. I do not pray that You should take them out of the world, but that You should keep them from the evil one*" (John 17:14-15 NKJV). We aren't *of* this world. We're living *in* it. The devil fights us because he hates God. Our bodies were created from the earth, but the real us—our soul/spirit—has an off-world origin. We come from where *God* dwells. Making Him our Home by dwelling in His Spirit here is really like going back to our roots. It's getting back to a state where our spirit is more important to us than our flesh.

The devil can't fight our spirit—he's a flesh devil; not a faith devil. He tries to assault us in the soulish realm (our mind, will, and emotions) by working against our flesh (the earthly part of us). He can only tempt you in the five senses. But when you've been attending to your spirit by dwelling in God and His Word, and when you've been building your faith in Him more than what you see all around you, your spirit begins to totally outweigh your flesh in terms of rank. When you're going through life that way, you're way more of a threat to the devil—and you're way less swayed by his manipulative temptation tactics.

You can get so powerful that the devil doesn't want to mess with you much. He messed with Jesus during the temptations, and the Word says the devil left him for a season (Luke 4:13). Why did Satan leave him for a season? Because he had enough of messing with the Power in Jesus that was greater than him! Guess what? You have a greater Power in you, too! Greater is He Who is in YOU than he that is in the world (1 John 4:4). The Hidden Help ministered to Jesus after the temptations, too.

So, not only did Jesus defeat the devil when tempted, but the angels in charge over Him came to His spiritual aid afterwards—they ministered to Him spiritually, helping to restore Him from the battle. The Hidden Help will do the same for you. That's one thing they're here for. Don't you just appreciate these "regular" angels? Aren't you thankful to God that He blessed us with such good Hidden Help?

What God has done for others, He will do for you (Acts 10:34). I want you to know that you can be safe under the shadow of the Almighty, knowing He's put an angelic force on this earth that is anything but regular! Legions of supernatural beings, who are invisible to you, know that you come from the same place they do—God's place—and they are not just willing but honored to serve God by fighting, safeguarding, and ministering to *you*. Glory!

You know, there's no telling how many times angels have saved and will save you from destruction during your life dwelling in the secret place of God. There have likely been many times that He has saved you from harm and you didn't even know it. His wonderful "regular" angels may have guided you out of harm's way without you even realizing it, or directly fighting the fallen ones tasked with trying to steal, kill, and destroy you (John 10:10). They work for Satan just like God's angels work for Him.

It doesn't matter what the devil does or how much he fights—we win in the end! And when you get to Heaven, go ahead and see for yourself. Ask the Lord to roll back the tape, so to speak, so you can see just how much He and the angels did to help *you*. Glory!

CHAPTER 9

THE WARRIOR
AND THE MESSENGER:
ARCHANGEL MICHAEL
AND GABRIEL

We serve a God of order and it shows up in the angelic host. Angels serve God in all sorts of ways, but the only two specifically named in our Bible are Michael and Gabriel—and when these two come, they don't seem to hide! Michael is a warrior. He's a fighter and the only angel specifically called an archangel in the Bible—which isn't a type of angelic being, but most people believe it's more of a title, showing rank over other angels.

Gabriel is probably the most famous in the Bible—he is called The Lord's Messenger, and his name means "God is Great." The Bible never specifically calls him an archangel, but because most consider him equal to Michael, many believe that he is one. Every time Gabriel shows up, he brings a message critical to the plan and purposes of God.

Many people believe that there are more archangels than Michael. They include Gabriel, and consider John's vision in

Revelation 8:2 as evidence that there are seven: *"And I saw the seven angels which stood before God; and to them were given seven trumpets."* From this, even though it's not plainly told to us in the Word, many believe there are seven of these angelic leaders, called archangels, who stand before God receiving commands that deal with Heaven and Earth.

When Satan was Lucifer, he was called *"the anointed cherub that covereth"* in Ezekiel 28:14, and many believe he was an archangel too, due to his high position over the throne, reflecting glory back upon God. There are even theories that maybe Michael was given Satan's rank as an archangel in Heaven once he was kicked out. I don't know about that! But, one thing is for sure when it comes to archangels: what we *don't* know about them could fill a book! Some things are mysteries to us, and this is one.

What we *do* know is that when Satan's rebellion broke out in Heaven, it was Michael who was mentioned by name as part of the war. *"And war broke out in Heaven: Michael and his angels fought with the dragon; and the dragon and his angels fought, but they did not prevail, nor was a place found for them in Heaven any longer. So the great dragon was cast out, that serpent of old, called the Devil and Satan, who deceives the whole world; he was cast to the earth, and his angels were cast out with him"* (Revelation 12:7-9 NKJV).

Years later on earth, Michael and Satan had another run-in over the body of Moses. Jude 1:9 (NKJV) says, *"Yet Michael the archangel, in contending with the devil, when he disputed about the body of Moses, dared not bring against him a reviling accusation, but said, 'The Lord rebuke you!'"* Michael knew Satan when he was Lucifer, back when he was so strong and powerful that he was given placement above the throne. Michael knew what it was like to go head-to-head in combat with him, too.

It's wise to notice that even as fierce, able, and powerful as Michael, the warrior archangel, was and is, even he knew that the best way to combat Satan was to rely on and use the name of the Lord. Think about it: If even the supernatural warriors of God know to use the name of the Lord, how much more should we use it in fighting our spiritual battles?

Never forget that God the Father exalted Jesus to a position of authority over all of creation, including the angels—and even when He was here walking the earth, even in His humanity, Jesus had the power to command angelic beings. The Lord has always been more powerful than the angelic host, and so using His name when confronted with anything Satan does in our life is the smart thing to do!

In the book of Daniel, as I talk about in this book, Michael is mentioned by a beautiful and majestic angel who told Daniel he'd been delayed because he was fighting a strong, fallen angelic being who was over all of Persia, which is now Iran. This prince of Persia, as he called him, shows us that fallen angels can take authority over regions. In this story, the prince of Persia was so fierce that the angel of the Lord couldn't get away without the help of Michael. This angel also mentions that after his time with Daniel, he was going *back* to fight that same demon over Persia some more! You see, the angels do battle! And some are more fierce than others. We know how powerful the archangel Michael is because he is not only the one who overcame Satan in the war in Heaven, but he also seems to be the back-up for others. The angel in the book of Daniel puts it this way: *"No one upholds me against these, except Michael . . ."* (Daniel 10:21 NKJV).

There's also a prophecy given in the book of Daniel that talks about the end times. *"At that time Michael shall stand up, The great prince who stands watch over the sons of your people . . ."* (Daniel 12:1 NKJV). This gives us an idea that the archangel

Michael doesn't just come to the aid of angels in battle, but he also stands watch over the children of God. Glory!

Now, Gabriel is probably the most famous angel mentioned in the Bible. He appears by name four times—in Daniel, chapters 8 and 9, and in Luke, chapters 1 and 26. The first time he appears, it's to Daniel with prophetic words about the future end times of the world. Daniel was living in a time when the Israelites were in exile in Babylon, but Daniel was a loyal man of God and stuck with his faith. He was a man who saw things in the spirit, and God gave him many prophetic visions of things to come.

One of the visions God gave him bothered him so much that this happened:

> Then it happened, when I, Daniel, had seen the vision and was seeking the meaning, that suddenly there stood before me one having the appearance of a man.
>
> And I heard a man's voice between the banks of the Ulai, who called, and said, "Gabriel, make this man understand the vision."
>
> So he came near where I stood, and when he came I was afraid and fell on my face; but he said to me, "Understand, son of man, that the vision refers to the time of the end."
>
> DANIEL 8:15-17 NKJV

Gabriel then proceeds to give a powerful prophecy of the end times that people are still studying and making predictions about today:

> And in the latter time of their kingdom, When the transgressors have reached their fullness, A king shall arise, Having fierce features, Who understands sinister schemes.
>
> His power shall be mighty, but not by his own power; He shall destroy fearfully, And shall prosper and thrive; He shall destroy the mighty, and also the holy people.

Through his cunning He shall cause deceit to prosper under his rule; And he shall exalt himself in his heart. He shall destroy many in their prosperity. He shall even rise against the Prince of princes; But he shall be broken without human means.

And the vision of the evenings and mornings Which was told is true; Therefore seal up the vision, For it refers to many days in the future.

DANIEL 8:23-26 NKJV

Gabriel comes back to Daniel again, after Daniel had been fasting and praying hard for Israel and himself:

Now while I was speaking, praying, and confessing my sin and the sin of my people Israel, and presenting my supplication before the Lord my God for the holy mountain of my God,

Yes, while I was speaking in prayer, the man Gabriel, whom I had seen in the vision at the beginning, being caused to fly swiftly, reached me about the time of the evening offering.

And he informed me, and talked with me, and said, "O Daniel, I have now come forth to give you skill to understand.

At the beginning of your supplications the command went out, and I have come to tell you, for you are greatly beloved; therefore consider the matter, and understand the vision:"

DANIEL 9:20-23 NKJV

Gabriel then goes on to give Daniel the famous "70 weeks of Daniel" end time prophecy that is still opening eyes today. You can read it for yourself in Daniel 9:24-27.

Gabriel the Messenger also brings a message about a child that would be the forerunner for Christ, John the Baptist. John would be critical to the ministry of Jesus, baptizing Him into the ministry and paving the way for Him by preaching, *"Repent, for the kingdom of Heaven is at hand!"* (Matthew 3:2 NKJV). Gabriel came to the priest, Zacharias, with the message that John would be born—even though his wife, Elizabeth, had always been barren, and by the time this word came, they were both old. God doesn't care about those things. If it's in His plan, it's happening!

> Then an angel of the Lord appeared to him, standing on the right side of the altar of incense.
> And when Zacharias saw him, he was troubled, and fear fell upon him.
> But the angel said to him, "Do not be afraid, Zacharias, for your prayer is heard; and your wife Elizabeth will bear you a son, and you shall call his name John.
> And you will have joy and gladness, and many will rejoice at his birth.
> For he will be great in the sight of the Lord, and shall drink neither wine nor strong drink. He will also be filled with the Holy Spirit, even from his mother's womb.
> And he will turn many of the children of Israel to the Lord their God.
> He will also go before Him in the spirit and power of Elijah, 'to turn the hearts of the fathers to the children,' and the disobedient to the wisdom of the just, to make ready a people prepared for the Lord.
>
> LUKE 1:11-17 NKJV

Zacharias didn't believe Gabriel, and he was struck dumb, unable to speak, until the baby came—the man couldn't say a word! That just goes to show, if you don't have anything good to say around Gabriel, you might not want to say anything at all. This is a powerful Messenger who only seems to come when there are critical messages to deliver from God Almighty.

The last message recorded in the Bible that Gabriel delivers is the most important message that he ever delivered—and not just for him, but also for the whole world. As believers, we thank God for it every day!

> Now in the sixth month the angel Gabriel was sent by God to a city of Galilee named Nazareth,

to a virgin betrothed to a man whose name was Joseph, of the house of David. The virgin's name was Mary.

And having come in, the angel said to her, "Rejoice, highly favored one, the Lord is with you; blessed are you among women!"

But when she saw him, she was troubled at his saying, and considered what manner of greeting this was.

Then the angel said to her, "Do not be afraid, Mary, for you have found favor with God.

And behold, you will conceive in your womb and bring forth a Son, and shall call His name JESUS.

He will be great, and will be called the Son of the Highest; and the Lord God will give Him the throne of His father David.

And He will reign over the house of Jacob forever, and of His kingdom there will be no end."

Then Mary said to the angel, "How can this be, since I do not know a man?"

And the angel answered and said to her, "The Holy Spirit will come upon you, and the power of the Highest will overshadow you; therefore, also, that Holy One Who is to be born will be called the Son of God.

Now indeed, Elizabeth your relative has also conceived a son in her old age; and this is now the sixth month for her who was called barren.

For with God nothing will be impossible.

Then Mary said, "Behold the maidservant of the Lord! Let it be to me according to your word." And the angel departed from her.

LUKE 1:26-38 NKJV

Gabriel the Messenger—from the father of John the Baptist, to the mother of Jesus, to the powerful words on the end times that we just may see come to pass in our lifetime, Gabriel is a revealer of God's plan for mankind. Every person he revealed himself to was awestruck and in shock.

Daniel became sick once and fell flat on his face on the floor another time, recording that he was terrified in the presence of Gabriel. Zacharias was gripped with fear, and was so shocked he couldn't even believe. Mary, the young virgin, is the only one who, while still afraid, seemed to keep her composure! Confronted with Gabriel, *"she was troubled at his saying, and considered what manner of greeting this was"*—which shows us that Mary was listening, yet was more unsettled by the words than by the supernatural being delivering them.

Mary is also the only one who had the last word with Gabriel, telling him to look at her—to behold her, the maidservant of God—and ending the conversation with willingness and a confirmation of her acceptance of God's Word to her. *"Let it be to me according to your word."* I think we could all learn a lesson from Mary. There's nothing more precious than simple faith and obedience—to be confident in God's plan enough to say, "Whatever you want, God! I'm here for You!"

CHAPTER 10

THE MYSTERY OF THE SERAPHIM, CHERUBIM, AND WHEELS WITHIN WHEELS

God created some fascinating beings, and here we'll discuss a few types of angelic beings that fall outside of what we think of when we think about angels. These beings are wild! Now, just to remind you again, just because an angelic being did something once and it was recorded in the Bible doesn't mean that's *all* they do . . . it's just all that God chose to reveal to us in His Word. Our place is here, for now, but one day when we reach Heaven, we are going to see these beings with our own eyes. So, we may as well get to know a little bit about them now.

And just remember that as strange and fascinating as these creations of God are, what we know about them is just a sliver of what we're going to learn about them and experience with them when we reach Heaven!

THE SERAPHIM
The Six-Winged Fiery Ones Who Continually Circle the Throne

Isaiah had a vision from God. He saw the Lord sitting on a throne, high and lifted up, and the train of His robe filled the entire temple. Above the throne were beings that Isaiah called seraphim (plural of a seraph), which means "burning ones" (see Isaiah 6). These beings are also mentioned in Numbers 21:6,8; Deuteronomy 8:15; and Isaiah 14:29, 30:6, but it's only in Isaiah 6 that we hear what this type of angelic being is called: seraphim.

The seraphim, unlike most angelic beings, have wings—six of them! They fly continually above the throne of the Lord in Isaiah's vision, praising God and proclaiming, *"Holy, holy, holy is the Lord of hosts; the whole earth is full of His glory!"* (Isaiah 6:3 NKJV). Two wings cover their faces, two cover their feet and body, and two are used to fly above the throne as they glide and swirl and continually give passionate praise to our God.

The root word *seraph* literally means "to set on fire, to burn," and it seems like these beings were created by God to blaze like fire. Closest to the throne that we know of, the seraphim are in the closest proximity to the immense power and glory of God's presence. They burn and can withstand His power, and yet they *still* cover themselves while they fly above His throne. Some say they cover their face out of reverence for God's glory and cover their feet and body out of modesty and reverence for God, too. But I think it might also be that they need to shield themselves from His immense glory and power. Our God is a Spirit and He is powerful!

The cry of the seraphim is done continually. When they say "holy," they aren't only talking about God's character as holy, as we think of holiness. That word in Isaiah 6 means "separated" and "unapproachable"—this shows us that the power of God is so great and so pure that His very nature requires some distance. Even the seraphim are set ablaze in His presence. *Holy* is a word we don't really understand today, but the angels understand that in its most pure form, the holiness of our God is powerful. God is set apart, or sanctified, by His very nature. His perfect purity sets Him apart from impurity.

Just imagine all the energy and power emanating from the throne of God. It could knock us dead in our physical body to be too close. Even the angels who were created to blaze around His throne recognize God's holy power. "Holy" is part of Who He is—and that the seraphim point this out continually shows us that the ones closest in proximity to God can't help but burst into praise in the presence of the Father. There is *no* God like our God! None!

In Isaiah 6, we see that Isaiah could not approach God until he was purified of all iniquity and sin. He was never asked of God to go and tell people anything until he was made pure before a holy God. It is through this vision—of what was required of Isaiah and what the seraphim continually proclaim (God's holiness/separateness)—that we are given information about God that gives us yet another clue that we need what Jesus gave us through His sacrifice. We cannot be in the presence of such a pure God with sin clinging to us—we *need* righteousness (right standing), and we have been given a Mediator in order to get it.

God Himself took the initiative in becoming our Redeemer. The sin-sick state we are born into because of the fall is like a wall that separates us from our Father—and God decided that no one but Himself could pay the price to break that barrier. By putting Himself in flesh as Jesus Christ, He decided that it was the only way we could be redeemed from what Satan had deceived us into becoming at the fall of man.

These bodies we now have since the fall are corruptible and cannot handle God's full awesome presence. To face Him directly would damage or even kill our mortal bodies. By sending Himself into the earth to be born a man, God really gave up Himself for us on the cross. As Jesus, He made His own blood the only acceptable sacrifice in order to wash our sin away. Purity for purity, He paid the price for us! That is why we can approach God now. We have free will and can deny Him, but if we accept Him, He uses Himself and His own blood to wash our sin away. There is nobody who can be a good enough person to withstand the holiness of God—we need redemption and salvation, and only the blood of Jesus can do it. God will accept nothing less than Himself as our Redeemer.

We aren't angels on assignment. We aren't servants who circle the throne. We are unique in all of creation—chosen sons and daughters of a God so holy, so glorious, and so powerful that He made a way for us to come boldly to His throne of grace in our time of need (Hebrews 4:16). Think about that! The seraphim fly above the throne covering themselves before a mighty God, but as His family, we can approach like kids running to their Father—without fear and without dread because He has already made things right. I'm telling you, if that doesn't tell you something about God's love for us, I don't know what will. Glory! I get excited just thinking about it!

God once walked in the cool of the day with Adam—it shows you how far we fell when sin entered mankind and this earth. Once, a man stood side by side with God and had no problems withstanding His power and glory. Through the sacrifice of God in Christ Jesus, it's a blessing to know that, one day, we'll be able to do that again! Today, we can go spiritually to the throne in prayer, but one day, when we exchange these bodies for incorruptible ones, we will once again be able to stand in God's presence, just like Adam once stood with God in the Garden. Until then, Isaiah's vision of the seraphim circling the throne and proclaiming the truth about God reminds us that our Father is matchless. In His power, in His glory, and in the love He has for us, our God is nothing short of awesome! It's no wonder each of those fiery seraphim circle the throne praising Him!

THE CHERUBIM
The Four-Faced Watchful Guardians of God's Throne... and More

When most people hear the word *cherub*, the first thing they think of are fat little babies with tiny wings playing little baby harps on clouds. That makes me laugh! Nothing could be further from the truth. The cherubim, which just means more than one cherub, are guardians. We're told that some of these guard the throne, and like all angelic beings, they move at the will of God (Psalm 99:1).

In Revelation 4, it is cherubim who are fully around the throne of God—and these beings are always guarding and moving around the throne. They move according to the Spirit of God, guard the place God sits, and act as watchmen for the throne. But not all cherubs stay in Heaven.

Other cherubs have been positioned as guards on earth, too. After the fall, it was cherubim who guarded the tree of life in the Garden of Eden to keep man from eating it and living forever in sin. It was also a cherub and a flaming sword, which turned every way, that guarded the entrance to Eden once man was driven out (Genesis 3:22-24).

Cherubim also guarded the Mercy Seat of the temple, which was located in a place called the Holy of Holies, another sanctum in the temple (Exodus 25:18-22, 37:5-7). When the Ark of the Covenant was built, God specifically ordered that two figures of cherubs were to be placed on either side of the ark, symbolic that the cherubim guard the place where God is. When King Solomon built the temple in Jerusalem, some of the statues he built were of cherubim, too. So, you could say that when God wants guards, the cherubim are the ones He uses for that job.

These angelic beings are fierce! The best description of them is found in Ezekiel, and they are by no means a pretty, little chubby-cheeked blond baby with a sweet little harp. That junk came from painters in the Renaissance period, when the Greek style was fashionable. It has no basis in reality when we're talking about the cherubim.

If you look in Ezekiel 1 and 10, you'll find that cherubim have four distinct faces all around their heads—they have the face of a man, an ox, a lion, and an eagle. Their bodies are not like a human but like a lion. Their feet aren't human-looking either, but are just like an ox, and they also have wings—four of them! Their wings stretch upward—two cover their bodies and two touch one another. When they move, they move straight forward wherever the Spirit of God wants them to go, and they don't turn as they go. They don't have to. Do you want to know why? It's because all of their wings are covered with *eyes*. That's right, eyes!

What are all these faces and eyes for on a cherub? The Word tells us that they're for seeing the works of God. That means these fierce angelic guardians are created to observe everything God does in every direction, all at once! That's not all. Like the seraphim that Isaiah sees, the cherubim that Ezekiel sees are also fiery beings. When they move, Ezekiel describes them like flaming torches moving through the air with something likened to the electric energy of lightning emanating from their whole bodies.

THE THRONES OR "WHEEL WITHIN A WHEEL"
To Me? The Strangest of God's Angelic Creation!

Now, along with the cherubim in Ezekiel's vision in chapter 10 are some other angelic beings created by God that are just plain hard to comprehend. Sometimes called "the thrones," but more often than not, they are referred to as the "wheel within a wheel" or "the wheels." You can find them in Ezekiel 1 and 10, and in Revelation 4. Now, the way Ezekiel describes them is wild! They are *so* different than anything else described as some type of angelic being, and yet nobody really knows if they are really individual angelic beings or if they are some kind of extension of cherubim that are used in certain situations. In Ezekiel's vision, these move in total sync with the cherubim.

They look like two huge wheels that intersect, and they spin constantly. They look like their name describes—a wheel within a wheel. Ezekiel described them as being so big that they reach from the ground to the top of the sky. You'd think these were machines if it wasn't also revealed in Ezekiel 10 that these wheels have the spirit of the cherub literally *within* them and eyes all around their wheels. Their eyes can see as they move. Isn't that mind-blowing?

The wheels also have wings—a pair on each side of them. When their intersecting wheels are spinning fast and their wings are flapping, Ezekiel said that the sound was thunderous. He compared the sound to armies of men moving, huge bodies of water moving, or even something similar to the voice of God Himself. The wheels see in every direction that their intersecting wheels spin.

Besides the wheels themselves, what makes them really different than other angelic beings is that Ezekiel describes them as being in total and complete sync with the cherubim. In his vision, it's revealed to him that the wheels are so connected to the cherubim that when the cherubim flew up, the wheels flew up. When the cherubim flew back, the wheels flew back. And when the cherubim stop, the wheels stop too and let their wings fully drop down. The wheels perfectly mirrored the movements of the cherubim, according to Ezekiel, and the cherubim move at the will of the Spirit of God. Do we serve a Creator or what?! This is wild!

So, what are these things? Who knows? All we know is what the Word has revealed. But one of the fascinating things to me about the wheels is that they don't just move with the cherubim, but they also hold blessings inside of them. Inside those wheels, there is what looked to Ezekiel like a burning center of spinning fire. At one point, the cherubim reach into those spinning intersecting wheels and remove blessings from God from their core. Whether this is literal in the spirit world or figurative, the point is made that these strange beings are also containers of God's blessings, which are distributed at His command.

Angels can take on other forms, so if these thrones or wheels are angelic beings taking on another form for the purpose of illustrating God's power, we do not know. But we do know that our God is mysterious and creative, and He can create whatever He wants. The thrones or the wheels are one more angelic mystery that we will one day fully understand.

Like all things with God that are beyond our grasp, we just have to take it on faith. We have to remind ourselves that we serve a God Whose thoughts are higher than our thoughts and Whose ways are higher than our ways. What He creates might seem unbelievable to our natural mind, but on the other side of this world, in the realm of His Spirit, these beings are normal, and one day we will see them with our own eyes. By then, after everything else God is going to reveal to us, who knows? The wheels just might be one more wonderful part of God's amazing creation—a buddy even to God's best guards, the cherubim.

CHAPTER 11

DANIEL: THE END TIMES SEER AND THE ANGEL WHO CAME FOR HIS WORDS

I want to share a little more about Daniel in this chapter and look at his experience with Gabriel from a practical standpoint. This chapter is about the power of *words*. Daniel had ethics and he's most famous for being thrown into the lions' den, and yet he was also visited by angels and given prophecies about the end times, which I believe we are living in today. When it came to the things of God, Daniel was incredibly loyal and faithful.

He wouldn't let go of the things of God, even under the societal and political pressure of his day. Like a bulldog clamping his chops on a bone, Daniel just wouldn't let go of what he knew to be right. Prayer was very important to Daniel, and so was fasting; but it was his *words*, the scriptures tell us, that brought angelic attention.

Words matter to God. Keeping yourself faithful to the things of God, even when everything and everyone around you is going the other way, is what's called the "narrow" path that leads to God. Lots of people take the wide path that leads to destruction. Lots of people truly believe that there is no real good and no real evil, and that it's all just a conditioning of the mind. So, they feel free to do and say whatever they want, as if there is no cost. There is always a cost. The wide path leads to destruction. The narrow path leads to life (Matthew 7:13-14).

This story of Daniel is a reminder to us that God sees and hears everything, and His angels respond to our words when they line up with God's. Daniel's end times visions correlate with those John had in the book of Revelation. Now, there are people who teach on the end times, but I'm not one of them. I believe that no matter what comes up in life and no matter what the devil does or his people do, all we as believers have to do is stay on course—stay on the narrow path, stay close to God, listen to the Holy Spirit, and follow the Word of God. This is how you "occupy" until the Lord comes (Luke 19:13). And you do that by living in faith, not fear.

Living in fear is playing into the hand of Satan. God has called us to live in faith in Him, not fear. Fear is an energy that draws more trouble from the enemy—because the fallen angels listen to the words of mankind, too. Like Job, what you fear the most can come upon you if you let that fear take over your mind. So it's very important to have faith in God, trust, and be at peace with Him, knowing that you are His, you are loved, and in the end, no matter what happens in this world, God will be with you and eternal life is yours. Remember, faith is the only thing that cancels out fear—and faith works by love . . . God's love.

So, let's see how words work to bring about angelic help. In the book of Daniel, chapter 10, Daniel had a vision that disturbed him so much that he fasted from everything pleasant to taste and prayed about it for three weeks. Then, one day during this fast, he was hanging around by a river with some people and God sent an angel to talk to him (verses 1-7). The scripture does not reference this angel as Gabriel.

Now, the angel that came wasn't seen by everyone; just Daniel. This is one way angels show up sometimes, just by opening your eyes to them—the veil is removed between you and the spiritual realm so you can physically see them. The Bible records that while nobody else saw the angel, everyone else felt his presence—and it scared them so much that they all got up to hide in the bushes. I have seen angels, but my wife has not. However, she says she has felt their presence and known they were there. We were created to feel the different energies in this world. Our bodies respond to all sorts of things, and so does our spirit.

The angel that Daniel saw that day amazed him. The angel was glowing, and dressed in fine linen and gold (verse 5). The angels in their authentic state are often dressed in what we would notice as beautiful garments—what this tells me is that if God sends His angels dressed nicely, why would He want you, His child, to look shabby? He doesn't! Holiness is about sticking to God's ways instead of the ways of the flesh, or of Satan—it is not about eschewing beautiful garments or things. It's a religious lie that in order to be holy you have to be plain or dressed shabbily. The angels of God are holy and they are magnificent. Don't let anybody tell you God doesn't care about beauty, because Heaven and His angels show us that God has no problem whatsoever with beautiful things.

The angel that Daniel saw had a face that was flashing like lightning. His eyes were blazing like fire. His body was like a sparkling gem, and Daniel said it looked like beryl. Now, beryl is a mineral that comes in many colors, but it's probable that it was the golden state of beryl that Daniel was talking about, since he next says the angel's arms and legs were bright like polished brass. He also said that the angel's voice was like that of a multitude of people talking all at once (verse 6). Can you imagine hearing and seeing such a being?

Daniel lost all physical strength when the angel arrived—the glory coming off of that angel affected his physical body. When the angel spoke, Daniel dropped and his face hit the ground. *Bam!* He flew on his face in the presence of that messenger from God because his physical body couldn't take the power. It just gave out. (verse 8).

The angel then touched Daniel, and the force of that one touch pulled Daniel right out of his state of being. The angel effortlessly set Daniel on his hands and knees (verses 9-10). Then the angel said, *"O Daniel, a man greatly beloved . . ."* (verse 11).

How would you like to have that kind of thing spoken to you? God sends an angel and says, "Oh Harry, greatly beloved!" Or maybe, "Shirley, Shirley, Shirley! The Lord just loves you, Shirley! You are greatly beloved by God!" Now, I don't have to imagine that because I know that I'm greatly beloved. That's not arrogance, that's just acceptance of God's love. I don't just *believe* He loves me, I *know* He does. You may say, "Well, who do you think you are?" I'll say, "I'm an adopted son of God! My Father loved me enough to send Jesus to die for my sins." Now that's love, buddy! Read what happened next:

> . . . *O Daniel, a man greatly beloved, understand the words that I speak unto thee, and stand upright: for unto thee am I now sent. And when he had spoken this word unto me, I stood trembling.*
>
> *Then said he unto me, Fear not, Daniel: for from the first day that thou didst set thine heart to understand, and to chasten thyself before thy God, <u>thy words were heard</u>, and <u>I am come for thy words</u>.*
>
> DANIEL 10:11-12

I want to deal with the part of that scripture where the angel said, *"I have come for thy words"* (verse 12). Words are powerful tools that can bring about a lot of change in the earth. But if you're not saying anything, then you're asking the Lord to make a trip for nothing! God comes to our aid when we use words . . . but not just any words. Our words must be words of faith.

God responds to words of faith. One thing we need to realize is that God isn't moved by need. He's moved by faith. There are a lot of needs in the world—all are caused by the corrupt influence of God's enemy and the resulting sin that brings about in pride, selfishness, cruelty, and mankind's inhumanity to one another. But God started this thing out right. There was a time when man was pure and walked with God in the cool of the day. There was a time on this earth before sin, before sickness, before selfishness and cruelty. The paradise of Eden wasn't wonderful just because it was a nice garden—it was wonderful because there was no evil permeating it. It was essentially a bit of Heaven set aside just for God's unusual and new creation: mankind.

However, mankind messed up and invited evil in, and since then, there has been a slow and continuous compression of sin on this planet that has affected every part of it. We are all the creation of God as well as the children of the original sinners on this planet—Adam and Eve—inheriting the sin nature on a spiritual level, and perhaps even on a physical level. The important thing to realize is that we were born into rebellion—and every single one of us entered this world amidst spiritual warfare.

But God made a plan through Jesus Christ. Satan would never give himself up to help anybody—he is full of pride, and if he helps someone, it is only to further his cause against God and Jesus Christ. Jesus, on the other hand, is God; Who left Heaven and came to live as a man and give Himself for man—to rescue that which was lost. The blood of Jesus matters in the spiritual realm. It's so powerful that it obliterates sin. It recreates the spirit of man. It is not a matter of works but of faith—and while it's hard to sometimes grasp, the truth is that our faith in God and acceptance of His Son is all it takes to recreate our spirit. Being born again gives us the only option out of the grip of what Satan originally brought into this earth. Being born again frees us on a spiritual level from the dictates of sin and sets us apart for the things of God.

If you are born again, you've been washed in the purity of Jesus Christ's pure and holy blood. God Himself is a pure and holy God. When He took on flesh and became a man, His essence permeated that blood through and through. Giving Himself as a sacrifice for us was pouring out something so pure and so holy that it had the ability to obliterate any sin in the line of mankind—any sin, any sinful state, and any iniquity at all. There is no state of being or act of man that the blood of Jesus cannot correct and make new.

The Word of God opens eyes, but it takes a spiritual change on the inside to really grasp its truth. This is why when a believer speaks the Word of God in faith, it is more powerful than Satan and all his works. It's why we can read it and absorb truth we sometimes can't even express—layers of spiritual truth that realign us with God's way of being when our earthly minds go off track. There is power in the Word of God. His words formed everything made—they have power. So, when we use the Word of God and speak it in faith, we are drawing from the energy of His power. That makes the angels pay attention, whether they are fallen or not.

We all want a good life. We may think of "the good life" in different ways, according to our personal views and preferences, but I've never met anyone who didn't think "the good life" was a joyful one, a peaceful one, a prosperous one, or an exciting one. The Word has everything we need for a good life. Still, nothing will get done unless we first take the initiative.

God did His part. He sent His Son and He sent His Word. Now it's up to you and me to speak that Word out in faith. Why? Because as we do, God will send spiritual reinforcements that we either may *see*, like Daniel, or *not see*, like those around him. Either way, that angel that day came for Daniel's words—because words matter in the spiritual realm, and they matter a whole lot more than you may think.

Remember what I said earlier: Angels don't follow just any word. They do what God asks them to do—and they are keen to bring God's Word to pass. Remember, they're helpers. And if we are speaking God's Word, the angels will take part in bringing God's Word to pass in our life.

This is not just about affirmations or confessions; this is about speaking the Word of God in faith. Faith is the missing element for a lot of people. They just vainly repeat things without actually believing them. Some people confess and never believe, so nothing happens. Some people affirm until they are blue in the face, and yet nothing changes. I'm not into that. I'm into possessing what I'm confessing—and letting patience have its perfect work until I am full and entire, wanting nothing (James 1:4).

Don't listen to those religious people who throw away faith and call speaking in faith a "blab it and grab it" heresy. They'd probably criticize Jesus if they had the chance! What they don't realize is that nobody taught more on faith and receiving than Jesus did. Some people can be so locked into their tradition that they can't let go.

Choosing to have faith in God shakes off the gloom and doom that fear sometimes brings. Choosing to have faith clears your mind of fear so you can think clearly—so your mind isn't cluttered with anxiety. Choosing faith allows your spirit to reign first place. Faith puts you in an atmosphere where you can hear the voice of God—so you can see His servant when he comes for your words. Glory!

I believe that God will come for your words, too. But if you are not saying anything of value, then the Lord won't make the trip for nothing! It is faith-filled words that will draw Him, not fear and doubt. First, you must believe that He exists— that His power is enough to save, deliver, heal, restore, and set you free.

Faith destroys all distance between God and man. It draws on the power of His presence within you. Unlike Daniel who lived in Old Testament times, we who are saved today have the very presence of God's Holy Spirit within us. He's that close to us!

When I say, "Hello, Jesus," He responds, "Hello, Jesse!" Why? Because He is close to me and He responds to my faith. What do I have faith in? His ability to hear my voice. If I didn't believe it, I would stop my own heart from hearing His voice. That's the way faith works.

God will respond to you . . . in the good times and in the desperate times. It doesn't matter if you're in a situation where nobody is nearby to help you, God will send one of His servants to help you if you're speaking words of faith.

Angels are servants of God, but you are a child of God and an heir according to His promises (Galatians 3:26-29)—and that's better! Angels work for God, but they respond to His Word. So if you're speaking God's Word, angels will get up and move! They will go to work to bring God's Word to pass in your life.

Now, if you read further in the book of Daniel, you'll find out that the prince of Persia withstood the angel. But the angel made sure to tell Daniel that he heard his words the first time. This tells me that we shouldn't give up. A delay is not a denial!

Don't ever let the devil tell you that God isn't listening to you. God hears you every time, but your words must be words of faith, and remember, sometimes there are things going on that you don't know anything about. There are spiritual battles going on, and sometimes the devil hinders an answer from coming.

The devil or another person might be able to hinder you, but no one can stop your answer from coming if you continue speaking words of faith. Faith will bring your answer home to you. This goes beyond believing. It's about knowing. The apostle Paul had a revelation of this. In his letter to Timothy, he said:

> *Whereunto I am appointed a preacher, and an apostle, and a teacher of the Gentiles.*
>
> *For the which cause I also suffer these things: nevertheless I am not ashamed: for I know Whom I have believed, and am persuaded that He is able to keep that which I have committed unto Him against that day.*
>
> *Hold fast the form of sound words, which thou hast heard of me, in faith and love which is in Christ Jesus.*
>
> *That good thing which was committed unto thee keep by the Holy Ghost which dwelleth in us.*
>
> 2 TIMOTHY 1:11-14

Knowing and believing are two different things. When you know something, you're confident about it. Paul knew God. He didn't just know about God; he was persuaded that God was able to fulfill His promises. So he held fast to words of soundness, and he did it in faith and in love. He called it a good thing!

Personally, I've moved beyond *believed* and now I am in the *knowing* part. It might seem crazy to other people, but I know what God can do and will do when I put my faith in Him and speak sound words. So I don't mind looking and sounding crazy sometimes because I'd rather have faith and see God bless me! When I speak in faith and love, I know I can expect results . . . and so can you.

Why are your words powerful? Because you are powerful. Whether you realize it or not, the very thing that makes you alive is the breath of God Almighty. Your body is just dust from this earth. But the combination of your spirit and soul is the real you—you got that part from God!

The Bible tells us that man was made in the image of God. He is a triune being. God is the Father, the Son, and the Holy Ghost. You are the spirit, soul, and body.

When God created man, He was just doodling and playing in the dirt. The original Hebrew text says He had one big lump of dirt. God began to sculpt and create a body out of the lump—fastening every vein, bone, muscle, and organ out of the earth.

So what did man look like after God got finished sculpting? Stiff . . . like a mannequin! There was no life present. Now, the sculpture was detailed and perfect in every way—we're the best art this world will ever see! And yet, as perfect as God's mannequin was, it was still just a lifeless piece of earth.

Then, God did something amazing. He took that earthen sculpture of a man and brought it right up to His face—and blew! He breathed into the man's nostrils and, *Wham!* Life went into that body!

Notice that God didn't breathe into the mouth. That would have been CPR, and God wasn't trying to resuscitate the boy! He was giving man life for the very first time. When God blew, the mannequin-looking sculpture became a living, breathing, and speaking spirit!

Man's eyes blinked open and the first thing he saw was the face of God—up close and personal. Suddenly, man started living, moving, breathing, and speaking. Man actually used the breath of God to live. *"For in Him we live, and move, and have our being; as certain also of your own poets have said, For we are also His offspring"* (Acts 17:28). Before God breathed into man, he could not speak. But afterwards, man was commanded to speak.

First, God told man to be fruitful, multiply, replenish the earth as it was needed, and subdue anything that got out of line. By telling him to subdue, God was warning Adam about the snake that was coming. Then, God told man to plant seed and reap the harvest—to live off of his sowing. He also gave man all power and authority over all the works of His hand.

Then, God said, and this is my paraphrase: 'Time to work, Adam! You're going to help Me today.' God gave man a job that required him to name every living thing.

What was God saying? He was saying, 'Speak, spirit! Call it, and it will be done!'

Have you ever seen a carousel with painted wooden horses? We have an old carousel here in New Orleans in City Park. There are painted horses that sit on a metal circle and go round and round. One horse might have a hoof up in the air, another will look like he's in mid-prance, but neither one of them are going anywhere. They're just sculptures—beautifully painted, but not alive.

In the beginning, all the animals were lifeless. God created a horse out of the dust of the ground, but it was a lifeless creature—and the Bible never records God picking up horses and chickens and breathing life into their nostrils. Why? I believe it's because He didn't do it. Instead, I believe that He chose another way. I believe that God chose to include Adam in the creative process when He told him to speak names over the animals.

Now, I know what you're thinking, "Brother Jesse has lost his mind!" I haven't. You might not believe me, but it's true. The Bible says: *"And out of the ground the LORD God formed every beast of the field, and every fowl of the air; and brought them unto Adam to see what he would call them: and whatsoever Adam called every living creature, that was the name thereof. And Adam gave names to all cattle, and to the fowl of the air, and to every beast of the field; but for Adam there was not found an help meet for him"* (Genesis 2:19-20).

Now, I believe that God didn't know what the names of these animal sculptures were. He just made them and He was counting on man to tell Him what they would be called.

And notice this: the Bible doesn't say God "made them to walk" over to where man was. It doesn't say God "told them to fly" or "convinced them to swim" over to where man was in the Garden. Why? I believe it's because they couldn't. I believe that God had to bring them over to Adam because they weren't alive yet. God's reason for bringing them to Adam? One reason only, *"to see what he would call them"* (Genesis 2:19).

What was God saying to man? "Speak, spirit!"

Now, I can't prove it happened like that, but you can't prove it didn't! I personally believe that God wanted Adam to be a part of creation. I think He wanted man to use the power of words, just like He did. Here's how I think it happened.

God brought the animals and, one by one, I believe He showed His creation to Adam.

"What do you call this, man? What do you say it is?"

"It is a horse!" And I believe that when Adam spoke the name, that's when life came into the animal. The horse breathed, opened its eyes, and then neighed for the first time. Then, God brought another sculpture and man said, "Lion!" The lion breathed, opened its eyes, and roared. Animal after animal, God brought them to Adam to see what he would call them—and I believe that's when their life began. One by one, Adam spoke life into their earthen bodies and they began to do what the Creator created them to do.

"Elephant!"—and the trunk went up.

"Eagle!"—and the bird took flight.

"Ram!"—and the horns lifted high in the air.

"Rhinoceros!"—and the rhino took off for the nearest pond.

"Bear!"—and the bear stood and roared!

Now, you might not agree with this scenario of creation and that's your right. None of us will know exactly how it happened until we get to Heaven, but that's what I personally believe happened after reading this passage of scripture. I believe that God was teaching man right then and there the power of his words.

I want you to realize how powerful God originally made you to be. You are a speaking spirit, a being formed of the earth in the very image of God, and you have His very breath inside of you now—breath that you should use to speak life.

You have to make speaking words of life a lifestyle; not a once in a while thing. Life needs to be your habit. You see, when God talks, life happens. This world came into existence because of the words of His mouth. It's a mystery how He did it all, and I believe that when we get to Heaven, God will bring Genesis to life for us by showing us how it all came to be.

But we don't have to see it to believe it's true. It's actually better that we just have simple faith in God's Word because that ought to be enough. God's Word is powerful and it has always been here. The Bible tells us, *"In the beginning was the Word, and the Word was with God, and the Word was God. The same was in the beginning with God. All things were made by Him; and without Him was not any thing made that was made. In Him was life; and the life was the light of men"* (John 1:1-4).

When God said, *"Let Us make man in Our image"* in Genesis 1:26, He was referring to more than just creating a triune being. He was referring to lifestyle, too. God's lifestyle is to speak words of life. He intends that man's lifestyle will also be to speak words of life. As I've said, your words matter. Even death and life are in the power of your tongue (Proverbs 18:21).

God gave mankind some of His power when He blew the breath of life into Adam's nostrils. That same power of God dwells within you, and when you are saved, you are able to recognize it and have faith in it. It's that power that will rise up from within you and quicken your mortal body back to health if you're sick (Romans 8:11).

That power of God within you is what goes out to others when you lay hands on them in prayer. Your words become powerful because you are more than just a lump of dirt. You are uniquely created in God's image and have the life of God *in* you. You are a speaking spirit, and when you're speaking God's Word in faith, you are powerful!

Even unsaved people have power because the very life that keeps them walking around is still God's breath. Man can do a lot when he focuses on something! But without a knowledge of God and an acceptance of God's plan, man is spiritually lost and confused; he is without peace because he doesn't know his Maker.

Consequently, a spiritually lost man doesn't understand the power of speaking words of life. He may speak positively, but he is not using even a fraction of his power because he's without understanding about God's words of life—and they are the most powerful words of all. I'm all for positive speaking. It's sure better than being negative! But faith is much better than being positive. Positive words hope for change. Faith creates change! That's why I think accepting Jesus as Lord and Savior is the most important decision a person can make—it's the way to inherit eternal life, but it's also the beginning of a new way of living.

Jesus is the reason I'm alive today—because without Him in my life, I honestly believe that I'd be dead by now. Like I've said, I was a rock musician with a drug and drinking habit that was killing me. But when Jesus came into my life, He changed all that. He gave me joy, purpose, and direction for my life. He gave me good words to speak and cleared up my confusion.

You see, in order to wash away my sin, there was a sacrifice that had to be made. To redeem mankind from sin, somebody had to die, and that was Jesus Christ. He came to this earth and led a sinless life. He was innocent and as His blood ran down that cross, God accepted every drop for the remission of sins—your sins, my sins, the whole world's sins . . . if they'll accept it. After Jesus did that, the work of redemption was finished. Now, all that any person has to do to be saved is to call upon the name of Jesus—to believe with the heart and confess with the mouth that Jesus is Lord (Romans 10:9-13).

Although everything that has gone on from creation to now may seem a little complicated, there is nothing complicated about knowing Jesus and living His way. It's not hard. It's easy because Jesus did all the work! You don't have to go to the cross to give up your own blood for sin. All you have to do is speak from your heart and accept what Jesus has done. God's ear is tuned to hear your voice—and He will accept your prayer no matter what you've done, what you've said, or how you've acted in the past.

If you've never asked Jesus to come into your heart, all you have to do is pray in your own words, ask for forgiveness, and invite Him into your life—and like that angel in the book of Daniel, He will come for your words. And if you already know the Lord but have gotten off track and just need to wipe your slate clean, all you have to do is reach out to Him again. Ask for forgiveness for whatever is weighing down your heart, and He will come for your words, too. You are never too far away to come back home. Jesus is always ready, willing, and excited to hear from you.

Second Corinthians 5:17 reminds us that when we let go of our way and adopt God's way through Jesus Christ, we are changed and made new from the inside out: *"Therefore if any man be in Christ, he is a new creature: old things are passed away; behold, all things are become new."*

It's never too late to start speaking words of life. It doesn't matter whether you got saved a minute ago or sixty years ago—start a habit of speaking words of life. You're going to talk every day anyway, you may as well say something good. You may as well give the angels a reason to respond, because they are listening . . . and they will come for your good *words*.

CHAPTER 12

DAVID'S GIANT CHALLENGE AND DANIEL'S DEMONIC DELAY

David had a woman on his mind when he threw down the cheese and started mouthing off at a giant.

"What'll I get if I kill 'em?" he asked his brothers. Like a typical teenager, David was interested in making a little something on the side.

"The king's daughter, you fool. Now give us the cheese and bread Dad sent you here with and get out of here. You just came to see the battle."

Now, you don't tell a seventeen-year-old boy with his hormones kicked up real high that he is going to get a woman if he slays a giant and not expect him to rise to the occasion.

"You mean to tell me that I'm gonna get a woman? Me?"

"The king's daughter, yeah. But you? No. Stop gawking and go home."

David started daydreaming . . . *A woman? Man, I'd knock a giant out for one of those—and the king's girl at that? Take a look at that! Whew!*

David was the youngest of the family—the red-haired teenage musician who stayed on the backside of the mountain tending sheep and playing his own Psalmic version of "Stairway to Heaven" while his big, bad brothers talked of slaying giants, marrying the king's daughter, and wearing a crown. Sure, Samuel had anointed him with enough oil to grease an engine, but his father and brothers couldn't have cared less. They were happy to keep him on the mountain working with the sheep where they didn't have to hear his baaaallads. Ha!

But that day, David wasn't on a mission to simply bring food to his brothers; he was on a mission from God, and he had no idea that Israel's adversity was about to crown him king.

"Come over here and whip me if you can, you bunch of wimps!" the Philistine giant roared. David watched as the giant wagged his big, microwave-sized head at the Israelites. About a hundred and twenty-five pounds of metal gleamed in the sun as the giant waved his arms around and cussed everything from God to the ground.

David was appalled at his brother's lack of enthusiasm. "Are you going to sit there and let him pop off like that?" he asked his brothers, "Are you gonna let that uncircumcised Philistine defile the armies of God and cuss us like that?"

He could see it in their eyes, "He's a giant, David! Now get out of here so we can figure out what we're going to do."

But David wouldn't leave. He couldn't believe that his brothers didn't have the guts to walk out there and kick the tar out of Goliath. He started scanning the ground for a decent rock.

"You blankety-blank, no-good, trashy bunch of Israelites!" he heard the giant go on, "I defy your blankety-blank God and you! I curse your blankety-blank, too!"

He looked at his brothers and the nearby soldiers and could read their minds. *Uh, that's okay. Just curse all you want there, Goliath!* they thought as they stared at Goliath's big microwave of a head and thought of living another day. "Uh, you want to try fighting him next, Ralph?" somebody in the tent said. But nobody moved. Fear had them by the jugular, and they were practically soiling their robes trying to figure out what to do.

"Ahhh! You bunch of losers. You call yourself God's blankety-blank people, but you're nothing but a bunch of puny wimps. Come on over here if you're man enough, and I'll knock the blank out of you in a blankety-blank-blank second!"

David couldn't take it another minute. "I'll fight this idiot today!" he hollered.

His brothers shouted back, "Shut up! Go back to your stinking sheep and stop fooling around."

"No! I'll put him down! I don't see you guys walking out there. Why not give me a shot?" David said, as he thought, *Yeah, this giant cannot win against my God. And I get the king's daughter if I kill him . . . and it's legal! Dad can't take her away either because it's the king's rule!*

Now, his motive was wrong on one hand—the boy wanted a woman and was willing to die at the chance of getting one. He was probably already contemplating lyrics for his next song, "Ohhhh, my love, my darling, I've hungered for your touch . . ." and imagining her response, "Sing to me, David. Sing to me, David. You want to kiss me? Yeah, you want to kiss me. Come over here, David!"

But God noticed the anointing that was on David and said, "Here is somebody that will stand in the gap. Here is somebody that is not trembling back in the tent. Here is somebody that is aggravated that someone is cussing Me!"

All of a sudden, the anointing of God that was poured on David by Samuel rose up. Courage swelled in him, and although he couldn't fit the armor, he didn't care. He was willing to go out just as he was because he knew without a shadow of doubt that God was on his side. From his spirit came courage so fierce that it bypassed his mind, and David shouted out to the giant, "You come against me with a spear, but I come against you in the name of the Lord God Jehovah!"

To the others, it was a threat, but to David it was a promise. He grabbed a rock from the dirt, put it in his slingshot, and started swirling it in the air. David had been rocking on the mountain for years, now he was about to rock out a giant in front of all his big, ugly buddies. Goliath saw the red hair and recognized the stature. *A lousy teenager*, he thought, and laughed and shouted at the soldiers, "Is this whatcha' got, boys? You wanna throw rocks?" He shook his head, looked at David and spat, "I'm going to pick the flesh off of your bones, boy, and feed you to the birds!"

"Bring it on, big man. I am going to feed your carcass to the birds. I am going to cut your microwave-sized head off and play ball. You understand me? I want to let you know what's about to go down, you uncovenanted, uncircumcised, God-cussing fool!"

Now, I'll be over to you in just a minute, little lady, he thought as he considered the king's daughter, *Yep, just hang on, baby. I'm coming to getcha'!*

David began to run. Whirling his sling in the air, he ran towards the giant with all his might—the sling whirling harder and harder in circles.

Foom! David released the rock. The Holy Spirit guided it as it flew through the air.

Pow! It knocked the giant right between the eyes and he began to drop.

Thump! Goliath's big head hit the ground.

All the oxygen was sucked out of the air that day as the crowd gasped at the sight of the giant on the ground. David didn't wait. He kept running until he got to Goliath's body and climbed on his chest like it was a stage, hollering, "I said he would go down, and he is down. Nobody can come against my God and win!"

Suddenly, David reached down for Goliath's heavy sword, pulled his giant head up at the perfect angle, and started sawing away. Then, David grabbed the head by the hair, lifted it up for all to see and said, "Now this is how you get ahead in life, right here!"

This story is a paraphrase of what actually happened to David the day that he stopped being just a sheep-watching musician and started being Israel's king, as told in 1 Samuel 17:1-58. Although Samuel anointed David as king before the big event, it was really Goliath who made him the king in the eyes of the people. His triumph showed all of Israel the power of God's anointing, and what could be done if you are willing to trust God and stand up for righteousness.

You see, it doesn't matter how small or insignificant you think you are. If you are a believer, then you are a threat to the devil and all his works. Your adversity has the potential to crown you king, if you let it. But you've got to be bold enough to speak up and not take the devil's attacks lying down. Don't be like David's brothers who were sitting back in fear and complaining about their circumstances rather than getting up and putting up a fight. David's fight began with an inner indignation that a giant would have the gall to mock God's children. Your fight will begin the same way when you become indignant at the devil's attempts to steal, kill, and destroy your life.

When the devil attacks you and tries to make a mockery of your God, it's in your best interest to stand up and say, "Oh no you will not! You are coming against a child of God, devil, and I'm not standing for this."

Samuel anointed David; Jesus anointed you. David had a rock; you have *The Rock*, Jesus Christ—and your very salvation has given you the authority to put the devil in his place. When you allow God's words to come sailing out of your mouth, you're going to see that giant in your life fall to the ground.

Anybody can believe and confess Jesus as Lord and be saved. Anybody can speak the Word in faith and see results. Remember from the last chapter, God didn't create us to be silent—He gave us life so that we might speak words of life. He gave us authority so that we might crush the works of the devil.

Adam's first job was to name the animals, but soon enough the scripture records how God said it was not good for man to be alone, and a female was created. The fact that God chose man's rib to create her shows that He meant for females to be working side-by-side with males. What I want you to notice is that God called *both* of them Adam. Why? Because the female "Adam" was also created in God's image. She had the breath of life within her and she was a speaking spirit, too.

When God called the woman Adam, He was proving her spiritual equality. I believe He was saying exactly what He said to Adam: "Speak, spirit! What you will say will come to pass. The creative force that made My male live, breathe, and speak with authority is the very same creative force dwelling in you."

Now, I've met many women in my years of ministry that were treated like second-class citizens in the church. That should never be because, although the fall of man happened and the curse came into the earth, Jesus redeemed us from the curse and has made women and men equal in God's sight.

"... *There is neither male nor female; for ye are all one in Christ Jesus*" (Galatians 3:28). It is Christ that unites us. Some people don't believe that a woman should be able to preach, but I do. Eve was just a name that *Adam* used. God called them both Adam— He saw them both as *one*. So what am I going to do? Say that God can't talk through the female Adam? No way! Women are power-ful creatures, made in God's image and created to speak His Word with authority. They can feed us physically, so why can't they feed us spiritually?

Paul's book of Corinthians was a letter to a church that was out of line on many issues. Paul didn't hate women; he was just trying to bring some social order to the family and the church. There were many cultural differences, too.

Christianity was brand new and they were working out the kinks on order in the church services. Although the women were allowed in the service, they were separated by sex—men on one side and women on the other. These gatherings would have seemed very informal compared to traditional Jewish services. Some theologians say that if a wife had something to say to her husband during the service, she might just shout out across the church. Think if a woman in your church would see her husband across the sanctuary and stand up and go, "Psst! Hey, Harry! Ask Ralph where he got that coat."

If that were going on, the preacher would have to set down some rules, right? Paul even had to tell them not to speak with other tongues in the middle of the service, too. They'd just interrupt the message to pray in tongues. He had to say, "Look, you can't do that. Unless it's a word from God and there is an interpreter, keep silent." Was he saying we should never pray in tongues in church? No! He was simply giving direction to keep order.

When he taught women to "be silent" in church, it was a direct order to the Corinthian church because of their dis-orderly conduct. The church service wasn't a question and answer session, so he didn't want them to shout out. That would be applied if there were a problem with order in the church today. But it *doesn't* mean women shouldn't ever speak in the church.

Some men are afraid that a woman will "usurp" authority over them if they speak or preach better than they do. They use Paul's teachings out of context to fit their own egotistical views. The order of the family between husband and wife is for peace and order so things run smoothly. But the original Greek for the word "aner" that Paul used works for man *or* husband. The Greek word "gune" can be translated either woman *or* wife. Not every man was a husband, and not every woman was a wife. So you've got to look at the situation around the scripture to determine what the Bible is saying because, by all means, women are not second-class citizens in the Word, and to teach that is wrong.

There were women in the Bible who were called prophetesses, and the apostles recognized certain women by name that were in ministry. If you research, you'll find God often led women to say and do His will . . . out loud and in front of everybody.

So I say, "Girls, preach the Gospel! Sing the Gospel! Witness! Disciple! Do what God has called you to do." If some fool says, "I don't want you usurping authority over men," tell him, "I'm not usurping anything. I'm a speaking spirit and made in God's image. He has called me to His service and I cannot disobey, so take it up with Him!"

It took a woman to get Jesus here. His mother, Mary, was just a teenager when an angel of God showed up to tell her that she was going to have a baby. But even though she was young, God cared about what she had to say.

Remember that in Luke 1:30-34, you find that Mary found favor with God. But when the angel told her that she'd conceive and bear a son, Mary put the brakes on. She was a girl with common sense, and even though she was looking at an angel, she thought, *Whoa! Wait a minute. That can't happen. I haven't been messing around.* Then the angel said, 'The Holy Ghost is going to come upon you and you are going to conceive and bear a child. You're going to call Him Emanuel, which means God with us' (paraphrase of Luke 1:35).

What did Mary do at this point? She considered what the angel said and "spiritualized" her common sense by agreeing with the angel and speaking, " . . . *Be it unto me according to thy word"* (Luke 1:38). Jesus couldn't have been born unless Mary spoke a word of agreement. Even though it was God's will for her life, Mary had to say it was OK or it wouldn't have happened. What was God doing? Waiting for her words!

She agreed and, nine months later, Jesus was born in a manger. Was He poor? No! They had money for the inn, but there was no room for them. The place was jammed full. Still, Jesus had three rich guys looking for Him, and it wasn't long before gold, frankincense, and myrrh were placed at His tiny feet. And it all started because of words.

The devil doesn't agree with God's Word, so he just has common sense. But those who agree with God's Word and use it in their lives have what I like to call "spiritualized" common sense. Jesus displayed this when the devil came to tempt Him. The devil didn't recognize Jesus as Messiah and asked him, 'If You're really the Son of God, do something. Turn this bread to stone. Jump off the side of the mountain and see if the angels catch You—do something so we'll know it's You' (paraphrase of Matthew 4:3,6).

Notice that the devil asked Jesus to do something he could see. Why? Because he's not a faith devil; he's a flesh devil. He'd been trying to kill the Messiah for years and was wondering, *Is this Him? We messed up on the last ones. Let's make sure.* But what did Jesus say in response to the temptations? 'Get out of here, you low-class, fallen, angelic fool. I rebuke you! The Word says not to tempt God' (paraphrase of Matthew 4:7). Temptation after temptation came, but Jesus didn't cave in.

Jesus had spiritualized common sense and He wasn't about to perform magic tricks for the devil to prove His divinity. Instead, He chose to simply speak the Word. Why? Because He knew that in the midst of great temptation, only the Word would keep Him stable and secure. So He used it consistently.

Daniel spoke the Word, and that angel I shared about in the last chapter came for his words, too (Daniel 10:12). Do you know how old Daniel was when he had the vision? Ninety-two years old! You see, God doesn't care if you're twelve or one hundred and twelve—He'll come for your words because you are an important speaking spirit and He is moved by your faith. I just can't stress that enough.

Now, I have touched on this in talking about the archangel Michael in a previous chapter, but I want to share more about how spiritual warfare can affect our prayers. What the Bible says in Daniel 10:13-14 shows us that even if we are believing by faith and doing everything right, the Satan's fallen angels can interfere with our angels and delay what we are believing for. Remember what the angel who came to Daniel said after telling him he'd come for his words: *"But the prince of the kingdom of Persia withstood me twenty-one days; and behold, Michael, one of the chief princes, came to help me, for I had been left alone there with the kings of Persia. Now I have come to make you understand what will happen to your people in the latter days, for the vision refers to many days yet to come."*

I want you to understand that the angel of God was not talking about a flesh and blood ruler; he was talking about a demon ruler.

This is the nature of the ongoing war in the spiritual world. This passage lets us know that demons can delay what's coming to us, but they cannot stop it if we stick to our vision. A delay is not a denial. Sometimes, there's just a demonic force trying to block what or who is coming to you.

Why didn't the angel just give up? Why did he continue to fight, and even enlist help from the archangel Michael? Because *Daniel* didn't give up. The angels continued to fight because Daniel continued to speak. That's the lesson I want you to understand. When you are habitual, uniform, and consistent in speaking the Word, it will be an everlasting reminder to the angels to keep on coming.

God doesn't send angels for stupid words or words of doubt and fear. He comes for sound words of faith. That's why the Bible tells us to, *"Hold fast the form of sound words, which thou hast heard of me, in faith and love which is in Christ Jesus"* (2 Timothy 1:13). In other words, be passionate about holding onto those words—they're going to keep you secure.

I'm a secure man. My wife, Cathy, has been trying to get me to change my hairstyle forever. I said, "Cathy, I am going to tell you something and this is the last time I am going to tell you this. I am like God; I change not." It's a joke, but she gets the point. I don't care if my hairstyle is out of style. Who dictates that stuff anyway? I don't live my life for other people. And besides, that's just too much work. The world and its ideas can cause instability in your life. They flip-flop over what they think and believe from one day to the next, but God's Word never changes. So I stick with the Word because it changes not. I like what I like, and that's it.

Now, you can quote the Word all day long, but it's what is *in* you that will get the angels moving. Some people just *speak* the Word, but they don't *believe* the Word. It takes believing and speaking working together. "How do I get my mind and spirit to line up, Brother Jesse?" Hear the Word. Read it. Listen to it. Get it in your ears regularly so you can think right regularly. That's how you "spiritualize" your common sense.

Faith is a choice. You can say, "This may not make sense to the natural mind, but it makes perfect sense in the spiritual realm. I'm going to believe God because His ways are higher and better. God hears my every word. His angels will come when I speak His Word."

If your mind says, "That's not going to happen," don't listen to your mind. Speak, spirit! Let your spirit override your mind, and use your mouth to confirm it. Say, "I doubt that doubt! The Word says (insert the scripture for your situation)." Quote that scripture in faith. Don't give up. The truth of God's Word will stabilize you, stopping doubt and confusion in its tracks.

People are always asking me theological questions about this or that—they love to try to go off on tangents. I often find that they forget the main message of the Word. Before I know it, I hear them adulterating the message by mixing in their own negative ideas about this or that into the Word. Then they get all confused and come to ask me about it. My response is to go back to the Word and put the "spiritualized" back into your common sense—what does God say? What is the message behind the Word? Do not complicate what is plain right in front of your eyes.

When you've got the soundness of God's Word in you, you can reject those adulterations of the Word that come across your path. You can recognize the heart of the message and not be tossed to and fro by those false systems of religion that bring confusion. The pure and unadulterated Word brings peace and clarity.

Does God love you? Yes! Does He want the best for you? Yes! Is the devil fighting you? Yes! Did Jesus die to give you authority over ALL the devil's works? Yes! Is His Word enough to make the devil flee? Yes! Are you going to pick up your Sword and use it? Yes! If a delay comes, is it a denial? No. Can demons in the spirit hinder the speed of receiving what you need? Yes. Will your manifestation come anyway if you don't give up? Yes!

It's the Word *you* say that will put angels to work in your life. It's your consistency that will keep them coming when they are fighting spiritual battles. There is no need to give up on your faith in the heat of adversity. God is on your side. Sure, wrong situations happen in life, but it's the rightness of God's Word that will bring about justice. So a clear knowledge of right is essential, and you get that through reading the Word and focusing on God's ways of doing things. It's only by knowing what is *right* that you can recognize and expose what is *wrong*.

Satan is a liar. He's a mocker. He'll try to make you feel small and insignificant. But, remember, you can be like David—you can watch that mocking giant fall. You can be like Daniel—you can stare death in the eye and say, "I don't care what you do or say, I'm following my God." You can hear God's voice and be like Mary and say, "I don't understand, but I agree. Let it be done according to Thy Word."

Thank God for Jesus—He's your Savior, and it's through *His blood* and the *word of your testimony* that you will overcome (Revelation 12:11). Notice that you need both. So, whatever you're believing God for today, speak the Word. Be consistent. Be passionate. Remember that God hears and angels do, too. They are His servants and they are on the way! They may have to bust through the devil's blockades and deal with spiritual forces that you know nothing about—but they're coming. What you *say* keeps them on the way! Speak the Word.

CHAPTER 13

"IMPOSSIBLE TO LIVE" ACCIDENT AND THE HAND OF HIDDEN HELP

One of the greatest memories I have of angel intervention in my own life happened when I was just a teenager. I was raised in the church. I'd played music since I was a very small boy, both in the church and on the street with my dad when he was witnessing. Back in those days, it was common for people to street witness, and it was also common for kids to be used for praise and worship. Still, even though I was surrounded by a lot of religious talk, it didn't really get into me. I believed in God, but I really didn't care about what I called "God stuff." I was rebelling, doing whatever I wanted to do, not giving a second thought about God, and yet He was still looking out for me . . . protecting me even.

I attribute God's hand of protection on my life to my mother, who prayed for me *all* the time. One night, she had a dream about me that she said wasn't just some normal dream. My mother, like many women who are close to God, knew the difference between regular dreams and when the Lord was showing her something. Mama said that in her dream, she saw me on a beach and the blood of Jesus was rushing over my body like a tidal wave—it was just flowing over me, closing in all around me and completely covering me. She told me, but I just didn't want to hear about it.

That dream happened the night before I borrowed my girlfriend Doris Roberts' car and found myself speeding down a small two-lane road in Bourg, Louisiana. It was raining hard and there was nobody around on the road that I could see, except for me and the man in front of me who was driving slowly. He was going like 35 mph and I wanted to do 65 mph. So I looked ahead of him into the other lane to see if there were any on-coming cars, and like any crazy teenager, I flew to try and pass him.

I've told this story before, and don't always talk about this man because I guess it doesn't matter—but he was a real jerk! When I sped up, he did too. He didn't want me to pass him. So I gunned it, and he did too. He wouldn't let me go around him. I was mad! I slowed down so I could get behind him because I was scared an on-coming car was going to come, but he didn't want me to do that either. That man slowed down so that I couldn't get back into the lane behind him, and do you know what he did? I can see it like it was yesterday. He was holding me in that other lane in the rain, but I could see his face and he just smiled at me. I can still see that smile today. He was keeping me in the lane where on-coming cars might come.

I hit that accelerator as hard as I could and got to about 68 mph to try and overtake him and pass him, and that is when the engine on that old car just died . . . and then I suddenly saw a pair of headlights coming in my direction. Now, remember, at the time I had originally tried to pass him, before he started playing games with me and not letting me out of the on-coming lane, there was nobody on the road and there was no on-coming traffic. When I saw those headlights coming in my direction, I panicked. I didn't know what to do. The car was still moving, even though the engine was dead because of how fast I'd been going. So I just hit the brakes as hard as I could, hoping that maybe, somehow, I could slide behind the smiling man before that oncoming car hit me head-on . . . but that is not what happened.

When I hit the brakes on Doris' car, the car fishtailed and started sliding all over the road. I barely missed that on-coming car, but then I had a whole other problem because I slid all the way across the street towards a ditch, and one of the wheels hit a cement culvert. Buddy, when that happened, I started flipping— and that's when something happened that showed me there was some Hidden Help in that car.

The car flipped three times, end over end, and during that time, everything in that car started to crumple and crack and break. I saw a mailbox come under the car and that's how I knew how high I was—because it was a six-foot mailbox and I cleared it. Even the steering wheel broke off in my hand, and when it did, I saw popcorn. It went flying everywhere and I was so surprised by that. During those flips, I felt like I was in an accordion instead of a car. I saw the passenger door fly open and crumple back in again, and there was this long piece of jagged steel that was coming from that area straight towards my side. It was going to punch a hole right through me. It was like I was seeing it in slow motion . . . and that's about when I felt a *hand*.

It was as if a real person with a big, heavy hand was with me in the car, and I felt that hand push hard against my right shoulder—it was pinning me to the seat. Before, I had been flopping around, but now I was being held. I was still moving, of course, but it was literally keeping that jagged piece of steel from impaling me.

When the car stopped, it was upside down. Slowly, I felt the weight of that huge hand on my right shoulder lift off of me, and as it did, I looked at my right shoulder and lifted it up and down on my own. I lifted my left shoulder too, just to check. I couldn't see anything holding me or letting me go, but as it released me I slid slowly and ended up against the door and roof . . . with that jagged piece of steel that should have killed me right at my side. I looked at my right shoulder again. Nothing. I looked at my left shoulder too. Nothing. No hand was visible. I knew that something supernatural had just happened to me and for some reason, I was fascinated by the popcorn.

I never did see that man again, the one who was playing games with me—he must have just kept on going when he saw me sliding. But I will never forget that smile. The rain was still falling pretty hard and I was trapped in the car, but it wasn't long before the police and an ambulance showed up for me. I was stuck but alive. Meanwhile, the traffic on the little road in Bourg, Louisiana had begun to build. It was taking them time to clear debris and to get me out, so traffic was down to one lane . . . and guess who was in it? Mama. Later, she would tell me that she had gone home and told my daddy about it, and asked him to pray.

She passed me up on that road, never knowing it was me because I was in a borrowed car. So, while they were at home, I was getting freed. It took a while to get me out. The car was so crumpled that they had to cut through the metal with a welding torch and use the jaws of life. But as they were pulling me out and getting me into the ambulance, I just kept hollering, "There's popcorn in there! Popcorn!" I kept trying to talk to them, but nobody was really listening. They thought I was in shock. I kept saying, "Listen! Somebody grabbed me! Somebody's hand was on my shoulder! I would have died otherwise! I was flying!!!"

Nobody paid attention. Maybe they thought I had internal injuries because I didn't look beat up at all, but to them? I was talking crazy. It wasn't until I was at the hospital that my parents were informed and they came to see me. We talked about it and I can remember Mama asking me questions, wondering if I'd felt anything in the car with me. I remember saying, "Mama, popcorn came flying out of that steering wheel. Mama, I felt like somebody had grabbed my shoulder."

Mama put two and two together then and said, "That was the tidal wave of the blood covenant in the dream I had the other night! God was protecting you! He was holding you down in that car so you wouldn't die and go to hell! You had better thank God that I'm praying for you, boy!" Mama was always dramatic like that. She was always on me about turning my life over to God—she prayed for me all the time, and she was the only one I told who believed me about the hand holding me and keeping that jagged steel away from me. Everybody else thought I had just been in shock. With that car flipping and everything breaking, they all figured I was in such shock that I imagined a hand holding me and imagined popcorn flying. But I knew that I hadn't been in shock. I just knew it!

The doctors checked me out and I left that hospital the same day. All I had was a little bitty cut over one eye and another cut on my hand that was about a half of an inch long. I'm telling you, nobody who saw that car could believe I survived in it. In fact, the next day there was a story about my accident in the newspaper. I made the front page! For a teenager, that was a big deal and I was excited. I can remember the headline to this day: "IMPOSSIBLE TO LIVE" in big letters.

I was worried about the car, but Doris' dad was kind to me about it. I told him how it stalled when I hit speed. I told him the full story, but he wasn't angry with me and didn't even make me pay him for it. It was an old car anyway, he said, and he was just happy that I had lived through the accident.

The day after the accident, when I woke up, I was so sore it was like my body had been put through the ringer. I was happy to be alive, but it still kind of irritated me that nobody believed me about the popcorn. I knew I couldn't prove what happened with the invisible hand, but I wanted to see the car for myself so that I could prove that I wasn't crazy. I knew that I'd seen popcorn.

"Daddy," I said, "I want to go to the wrecking yard and see that car for myself." So, he drove me out there and we talked on the way. I kept telling him, "Everybody thinks I'm in shock, but I know what I saw. Popcorn came flying out of that steering wheel!" Well, when we got to the wrecking yard, I was so sore it was hard to even get up and walk around. We waited and they picked up that car with a wench and set it down—and when we looked inside, guess what we saw? POPCORN. That's right!

There was popcorn all over the floorboard. Dad and I looked and looked at that car, and we talked about it. We ascertained that there must have been a bag of popcorn in the glove box and with the car flipping and breaking, the glove box must have popped open at the same time that the steering wheel broke in my hand. It looked like popcorn was coming out of the wheel because it was flying up at the same time.

The popcorn actually being in that car proved to me that I wasn't in shock at all. It proved to me that what I experienced happened—not in my head, but in reality. I saw that popcorn. I felt that hand. And the jagged steel that should have killed me didn't because there was some Hidden Help in that car.

Now that so many years have passed, I look back and do you know what I'm really amazed by? Of course, the hand of the Hidden Help, but also Mama. My mother's name was Velma, and she died at the age of 49 on Easter morning. She wanted to go Home, and so she did. She was ready. But during her time on this earth, she enjoyed using her faith. Mama was a strong woman who loved God and me—and it was that strength of will that kept her praying for me, pressing in, and even receiving dreams and visions about me.

When I didn't want anything to do with God, Mama didn't care what I said. She didn't let it get under her skin. She saw all my running from God as foolishness, and so she just prayed and stayed at it. She knew there was no place I could hide from God and her prayers. It was like I was in her spiritual crosshairs! The woman just wouldn't give up on me. It was just like she always told me, "Boy, it's just your tough luck you belong to me. You're getting saved whether you like it or not!"

Now, you'd think after I survived this wreck, I'd get saved right then, right? Wrong. I was as stubborn as my mama and I didn't want to listen. But in my heart, I *knew* God had protected me, and I knew He did it because I had a purpose of some kind and my mama was praying for me. Mama never forgot that she had the promise of her family down to a thousand generations. Never.

There's something to be said for stubborn mothers who care enough to speak the Word, pray, and believe that whatever the Word says is just flat going to happen. These kinds of women *believe*, no matter how wild their kids are! Mama was never scared to tell me the truth, even when I didn't want to hear it. She never thought I was outside of God's reach, even when she knew I was doing terrible things. She wanted me to know when God told her something or showed her something about me. I hated it, but it sunk into me. When I look back now, I think it was important for her to tell me that dream—it connected God's protection with that hand, and it showed me my mother was a part of that protective barrier over my young life.

On Easter Sunday in 1982, my mother went Home to be with Jesus, but I'll never forget how she was always the first one to the believe. The first to believe and not flinch. The first one to pray for me. The first one to believe that there was nothing I could do that God wouldn't forgive. The first to tell me and to always remind me that God was waiting for me.

It's a wonderful thing to stand in the gap for somebody. It's also a wonderful thing to see God work, to experience the power of Hidden Help, and to praise God for it. I learned from my mama to always give God thanks when He intervenes—to be quick to believe and quick to appreciate whatever God has done, or whatever God is doing. If He's moving, it's worth noticing and telling others about.

I hope you enjoyed this testimony of when I was just seventeen years old. I know I've told this one before, but it was so formative in my life and such a blessing for me to remember. I'm thankful whenever I get the opportunity to share what God has done for me because, well, He's real, and He moves in mysterious ways—but mostly, He's faithful. If He said He has given His angels charge over you, then be like my mama and just believe it!

CHAPTER 14

ANGELIC EXPERIENCES WON'T INSULATE US FROM THE ATTACKS OF THE ENEMY

Angels in the Bible often come looking like regular people, but there is something different about them—they may be brighter, appear out of nowhere, and sometimes leave in impossible ways, too.

There was a man in the Bible named Manoah who was married to a woman who couldn't have children. At that time, God's people were under Philistine control and one day, an angel of the Lord visited Manoah's wife. He looked normal to her . . . almost. And she might not have thought he was anything but a regular man except that something about his face looked angelic to her. It wasn't enough for her to know for certain, but there was just something different about him. This shows us that this angel was definitely taking on a human form, just like Hidden Help often do. But his countenance was still giving her clues.

She didn't ask his name. She didn't ask where he was from. And the angel in disguise didn't tell her either because he was there to deliver a message. He told the woman that her barren days were over and she would have a son who *"shall <u>begin</u> to deliver Israel out of the hand of the Philistines"* (Judges 13:5 NKJV). He even gave her specific instructions on how she should eat and drink while pregnant, too. *"Now, drink no wine or similar drink, nor eat anything unclean, for the child shall be a Nazirite to God from the womb to the day of his death"* (Judges 13:7 NKJV). She didn't know what to think. She'd been barren for years and still wasn't sure if he was a man of God with a prophetic gifting or an actual angel of God.

He left and that day, when she told her husband, Manoah, about it, he decided that they should both pray together for the man or angel to come back—and God answered their prayer. The angel returned. They were so excited. The angel repeated everything to Manoah that he'd already told his wife. Before long, the couple tried to offer the angel to stay for dinner. They wanted to cook a young goat for him, a delicacy that they hoped he'd like. The angel said that he wouldn't eat at all, but if they wanted to, they should offer it instead as a burnt offering to the Lord.

I want you to notice something about angels that this story illustrates so well. The angels of God will always lead you to honor God, praise God, or do something for God . . . they will never allow you to serve *them*. Again, it is their role to serve *God*—and if you are serving God, as His child, then they will help or serve *you*.

So, the couple prepared the sacrifice and they gave thanks to the Lord. The Word tells us that when they lit the fire for the sacrifice, a flame shot up very high on the altar. It went flying up into the sky, and that's when the angel leaped *into* the rising flame, shot straight up through the fire, and completely disappeared. There was no confusion about whether he was a prophet or an angel then! Manoah and his wife had just *"enter-*

tained angels unawares," like the scripture says. That's one big exit, isn't it? Their son would end up taking one big exit, too.

Do you know who their son was? Samson! And if you know anything about his life, you probably know that he was a devout Nazirite to God all the days of his life, just like the angel said he would be. Angels of God don't speak lies. When they give a prophecy or a directive, it's from God—and God is not a man, that He should lie (Numbers 23:19).

Samson grew and became famous for his strength. As a Nazirite, he was a devout man and lived just like the angel said he would—he drank no strong drinks, ate nothing unclean, and never put a razor to his head. His faith was bound up in his devoutness to God, and his hair represented his faith in Him. His strength came as a gift from God. You may or may not know the story, but I think it's got some serious wisdom we can all learn from.

Samson had a moral problem. Even though God's gifting of strength was on him, and even though he was devout to his faith, his moral failings hurt him in the end. He goes to Gaza, one of the main cities of the Philistines, and sleeps with a prostitute. Some Philistines in the city find out and try to surround him in the morning, standing charge by the city gates so he can't get out. He lays low until midnight, and then goes to the gate, rips it out of the ground, gateposts and all, and walks right out of Gaza with the gates on his shoulders.

Samson is cocky. As a devout man, he shouldn't have been going into enemy territory just to sleep with women, but his morality just wasn't in the place that it should've been. Not long after this incident, he meets a woman that he falls head over heels for in a valley area outside of Jerusalem. Her name is Delilah, and she's a Philistine too.

You see, Samson was playing with the enemy. He was messing with their women, and Delilah was a woman he should never have been messing with. You see, Samson's physical strength helped him do great things, but his moral weakness would eventually railroad his life—because, and I want you to hear me here . . . there's only so long you can play around before the devil trips you up and God removes His hand. God is merciful, but He is just. If you want trouble, just give into temptation over and over and it'll come!

The Lord won't bless what is wrong in His sight. Samson played around and fell in love with the enemy—but he never would have fallen in love with an enemy if he hadn't put himself in the position to do it in the first place! Ego will make you think that you can side with the enemy and things are still going to go smoothly for you. Wrong! Samson found out the hard way that he might have loved Delilah, but Delilah loved herself. She wasn't a neutral party. She cared more about herself and her own people than she ever cared about Samson, no matter how big, bad, and strong he was.

The minute Delilah was offered money to betray Samson, she did it. She would lie with him, sweet talk him, and manipulate him every chance she could. She wanted him to tell her everything so she could turn him in for money. So, she began to go after him hard, always manipulating their conversations and badgering him for the secret to his strength. Eventually, he gave in. He loved her, but was so exasperated by her questions that he broke down: "*. . . he told her all his heart and said to her, 'No razor has ever come upon my head, for I have been a Nazirite to God from my mother's womb. If I am shaven my strength will leave me . . .'"* (Judges 16:17 NKJV).

A lot of people just focus on Samson's hair, but what you have to realize is that his hair represented his faith in God— his Nazirite devoutness, which was something he'd been since the womb. Samson wasn't just naturally strong; he was imbued with supernatural strength from God, but it was only as good as his faith. To Samson, being consecrated to God as a Nazirite was who he *was*—it was bound to his identity. To Samson, to lose his identity in God was to lose his gift from God. So, he had faith in that hair. He really did believe that it was the secret to his strength.

I'm saying all this to illustrate a point: We are held accountable for the gift God gives us. Even an angel telling you what's to come doesn't mean the devil isn't going to fight you. You can't expect smooth sailing if you get cocky enough to plant yourself in the enemy's camp. Moral failing will always stunt your growth. It'll steal from you too, if you let it go on too long. Remember, the devil is always going to try and thwart God's plan. That's just a fact. As God's children, we are supposed to resist the devil, not assist the devil! The Word says if we resist, he will flee (James 4:7).

Samson didn't resist the devil and didn't reel himself in, and that made his life much harder than it needed to be. Maybe he got prideful about his gift of strength and started thinking he could do whatever he wanted. Maybe he thought he could straddle the line between what was right and wrong— that entering into an intimate relationship with the enemy was no big deal. I want you to know that God will never stop you from going in the opposite direction of His best. You and I have free will, and God won't force us to do anything. We must force ourselves to do what's right, even if what's wrong looks as good as Delilah looked to Samson!

Delilah betrayed Samson as quick as she could. The moment he revealed his heart and his weakness to her, she went out and called the Philistine men. She collected her money and then went back to set him up. She lulled him to sleep on her lap, and then called in a man to shave off the seven locks of his head so the Philistines could bust in and capture him.

Can you imagine the betrayal Samson felt when he realized what happened? Even while they were railing on him and she was screaming like she had nothing to do with it, Samson tried to fight back, *"But he did not know that the Lord had departed from him"* (Judges 16:20 NKJV).

Samson was a trophy for the Philistines and they were brutal to him. They gouged out his eyes. They took him to prison. They made him slave away as a grinder of grain. They'd take him out a lot and display him to the people. They loved making him perform for them blindly. They loved humiliating him because they loved seeing this formerly strong man come to such a low place.

Samson was the laughing stock of the Philistine people. Oh, but his hair was growing! He felt it, even blind as he ground the grain in prison. Samson knew that he'd never be free or see again on earth, but he had hope that he could still do something for God—that he could get back at the Philistines for taking his eyes. Samson wanted to be redeemed from his mistakes and have the hand of God on him again.

Do you know what? Samson was right to have hope. You see, God knows that even if we misstep, even if we feel totally lost, hope is never lost—and if we are humble and pray to God, He can make a way for us to continue our destiny even if it doesn't look like anything is going the right way for us.

The Philistines thought it would be a great idea to have a huge sacrifice to their god of grain and fertility to celebrate Samson's capture. At the temple, thousands came to be a part of the rejoicing. Samson was still grinding away grain when they dragged him up to the temple to make a spectacle of him in front of the thousands who'd showed up.

They were bringing Samson out to perform for the crowds and he asked to be leaned up against the support pillars. He told them because he was blind, he needed to lean against something. His guards agreed and they put him between the support pillars. All the leaders of the Philistine people were there for the show when Samson called out to the Lord. *"O Lord God, remember me, I pray! Strengthen me, I pray, just this once, O God, that I may with one blow take vengeance on the Philistines for my two eyes!"* (Judges 16:28 NKJV).

Samson didn't even pause to wonder if God heard his cry when he put his hands on two pillars, braced himself, and started to push. You see, his faith came back to him. *"Let me die with the Philistines!"* (verse 30) he cried out, and with one push, his gift came back to him. His strength was restored in a moment, and those support pillars began to move. Glory!

Samson took down that whole temple with one push. About three thousand Philistines and all those leaders bit the dust that day, and Samson died along with them. Now, Samson was a mighty warrior during his life. He'd taken down many Philistines in his fighting days. But in that moment, the Word says that Samson took out more of the enemies of God's people than all of his previous years combined.

What did losing the leaders and so many people do for the Israelites under Philistine control? Well, it began exactly what the angel of God told Samson's mother all those years before—it *began* Israel's deliverance. He didn't free them from Philistine oppression, but he definitely disrupted their power over the Israelites.

Angels speak for God. They are sometimes sent to help us physically. They are sometimes sent with advice on what to do and where to do it. Some are simply messengers. With his last push and his last breath, Samson made history when he took down that Philistine temple to other gods. Samson is listed with the heroes of faith in Hebrews 11:32.

The Hidden Help aren't always discreet, but we can be sure that if they've chosen to take on human form and speak, then they are speaking for our God—and what God says will always come to pass, one way or another. We all have free will and we aren't robots for God. We can go about our calling in many ways. We can take paths that make getting to our destination more streamlined or a whole lot harder.

Delilah was Samson's temptation—he fell for it and that choice brought destruction to his life. You see, God sent an angel to make sure his mother knew (and would later tell him) that he was meant to be set apart. Most who took the Nazirite vow of Numbers 6:2-21 did it for a short time, sort of like people do fasts. But the angel said Samson was to do it from the womb to the grave. That means he was always meant to be set apart—sanctified unto God—and that doesn't include playing around with women in the enemy's camp.

Remember that Samson was a hero for taking out so many of the Philistines. He wasn't a hero for sleeping with the enemy and getting his head shaved and his eyes gouged out. He wasn't a hero for grinding grain in prison. His heroics were in his strength—and his strength was the gift of God, which was intricately connected to sanctification and faith.

God's Word is full of direction and help for us so that we can be wise. The Deliahs in this world come and go. The enemies of God who mock His people are always around looking to trip us up. Pride and arrogance about the gifts God gives us can only set us up to fall—because pride can make a person feel invincible, and that leads to doing risky and ridiculous things. Buddy, pride can turn even the most gifted person into a fool!

Let Samson be a lesson. Don't mess with what you know isn't for you. Do right before God. Resist the devil; don't assist him. Don't get cocky even if you're super-gifted—because unless you find humility and repent, you just might lose the best part of your gift by playing around and acting the fool.

Bold confidence is good when used towards what's good, but it's terrible when you use it to dive headlong into situations you know are against your own faith. Samson thought he was so strong and gifted that even if he planted himself in the enemy's camp, and even if he fooled around with an enemy woman, he'd be OK. He still fulfilled God's plan for his life, but he also lost it in the process.

I think 1 Peter 5:8 (NKJV) says it best when it gives this wise warning: *"Be sober, be vigilant; because your adversary the devil walks about like a roaring lion, seeking whom he may devour."*

The devil is serious in his lust to attack God's plan and His people. And it doesn't matter how gifted you are, how powerful you are in your own strength, or even if an angel came down to talk to you twice just to tell your mama so . . . none of that will stop Satan from trying to steal, kill, and destroy your life. If the devil tempted Jesus, he'll have no problem tempting you or anybody else. So, be wise and vigilant, and don't take the bait . . . because *nothing* he offers is ever worth the loss.

CHAPTER 15

From Lucifer to Satan: Rebellious Angels, Mankind's Fall, and Overcoming in Jesus

Whether you call them fallen angels or demons, or anything else, these spiritual beings were once God's angels. They're fallen, but they are still powerful, intelligent, and can move in and out of our world like the other angels do. They are evil and influencers of all that is evil in mankind, and do their work both on this earth and in the heavenlies. They don't sleep, or need rest, or even eat that we know of—and just like Satan, they were kicked out of Heaven, too. Many are here on earth and some are chained and held captive, but all are in line for God's wrathful judgment at the end of time.

God created the angels with free will, like us. If they didn't have free will, Lucifer would never have been able to rebel, and one-third of Heaven's angels would never have rebelled along with him (Isaiah 14:12-15). While God's holy angels don't veer from their love and loyalty and exist to serve God, the fallen angels live by a destructive, God-hating agenda, rooted in what got them to reject God in the first place: pride and a lust for power, glory, and God's position.

If God's angels are the Hidden Help, Satan's are the opposite. They want to disrupt God's plan for mankind and make us just like them, and they do it simply because they are in war with God. I believe they hate the fact that He loves us, that we were given so much, and that we were made to be Family—and everything they do to us is just to hurt God. If God's angels are ministers unto salvation, then Satan's angels are ministers unto damnation. They're always working to influence this earth their way—away from God, His Word, and all that He stands for.

When Jesus was still in His mother's belly, God's angels came to shepherds and told them where He would be born. And just at the proclamation of His soon coming birth, the Word says a multitude of God's angels filled the sky and began to proclaim God's message: *"Glory to God in the highest, and on earth peace, good will toward men"* (Luke 2:14).

You could say that the fallen angels have the opposite message of Luke 2:14. They seek to deny and dismiss the glory of God, and get people to do the same. They aim to hurt God in Heaven by creating turmoil on earth, and get people to do the same. And regardless of what they say or how they make their motives appear, they have nothing but ill will toward mankind. Every demon or fallen angel is part of Satan's rebellion, which began in Heaven.

We call him Satan. Before he rebelled, he was called Lucifer, which means "Light Bringer," and he was the highest ranking angelic being in all of Heaven. He was the most beautiful of all of God's angelic creations, with piped instruments literally as part of his body, and precious stones covered him. He was called the anointed cherub, a covering cherub, and in his original form, he was the most majestic and grand angelic being God ever created (Ezekiel 28, Isaiah 14). Positioned above the throne, his role as a covering angel was to reflect the glory of God back onto the throne.

We don't fully know why he fell into the sin of pride and iniquity; the Bible just says that his heart became prideful because of his own beauty—that he looked at his own splendor and got prideful, corrupting his wisdom in the process (Ezekiel 28:17). He became totally self-absorbed instead of God-absorbed. He wasn't content with being the highest ranking and most beautiful angelic being God ever made—he wanted more. Lucifer wanted to be like God, and to be praised and glorified, too. The sin of his pride corrupted him and, eventually, he led a full-on rebellion.

We don't know how long it took for Lucifer's pride to get to the point of action, but the Word describes that his fall from Heaven started with words. They're called "The Five I Wills," and you can find them in Isaiah 14:12-15:

> How art thou fallen from Heaven, O Lucifer, son of the morning! how art thou cut down to the ground, which didst weaken the nations!
>
> For thou hast said in thine heart, I will ascend into Heaven, I will exalt my throne above the stars of God: I will sit also upon the mount of the congregation, in the sides of the north:
>
> I will ascend above the heights of the clouds; I will be like the most High.
>
> Yet thou shalt be brought down to hell, to the sides of the pit.

You know, that last verse is the one you should concentrate on because that's exactly where all those "I Wills" are taking that fool! No angel can compete with God for glory, power, or control and actually win. No angel can rebel against God and expect it to end well. As human beings tempted by

Satan, we've been given a Redeemer in Christ Jesus—so even if we go astray, we have a way back through God's mercy and grace. Satan had no tempter and created the corruption inside of himself, and so he has no way back. There is no redemption for him. There's only judgment waiting for him, and so now he knows he's got nothing left to lose. I believe we are living in the end times, and he is increasing his assaults on mankind in the spirit because he knows his time is short (Revelation 12:12).

Satan knows God's Word. Maybe he knows it better than most Christians! He knows what the Word says will happen to him, but he doesn't seem to care. In his corrupted mind, he's still trying to win in some way. He wants to take as many of us, God's beloved, as he can and pull us along with him into that final place waiting for him—the pit of hell.

While Christianity (the time of grace through Jesus Christ) began a little over 2000 years ago here on earth, Jesus saw when Lucifer was kicked down to earth. He said, *"I saw Satan fall like lightning from Heaven"* (Luke 10:18 NKJV). Notice the reference to light as well as the name change. The name Satan simply means accuser and adversary.

Revelation 12:7-9 tells us how it happened: *"And there was war in Heaven: Michael and his angels fought against the dragon; and the dragon fought and his angels, and prevailed not; neither was their place found any more in Heaven. And the great dragon was cast out, that old serpent, called the Devil, and Satan, which deceiveth the whole world: he was cast out into the earth, and his angels were cast out with him."*

Even today, Satan still wants to be seen as Lucifer, the Light Bringer. He wants to be praised and worshipped, and seen as an enlightener. The scriptures tell us that he often comes as an "angel of light" to deceive humanity. All you have to do is look at the state of the world today to see the effects of his "enlightenment"—and those lies began with the serpent and Eve in the Garden of Eden.

Once on earth, Satan set out to turn God's beloved creation to his own twisted and rebellious mindset. He'd already persuaded one-third of Heaven's angels to abandon their faith and join him while still in Heaven, and he wanted mankind here on earth, too. So, he began with the woman, Eve. The Word says he came to her as a walking serpent—because Satan, like all angels, can take on any form he wants.

Eden was paradise, and both Adam and Eve knew no sin. They lived like Heaven on earth—the work they did was easy, and they didn't work by the sweat of their brow for anything. Life was abundant and rich, and they were completely sinless, only knowing good. They had no concept of evil and were immortal. But they did have free will. The Garden was full of all sorts of trees, but God placed a particular one in the center, and He called it "the tree of the knowledge of good and evil." He commanded them *not* to eat of it and warned them that if they did, they would die—they would move from immortality to mortality.

At that time, nothing stood between God and His creation. There was no sin or iniquity. And God often came down and walked in the cool of the day with them. In Genesis 1:28 it tells us that God blessed them, told them to be fruitful, multiply, replenish the earth, and subdue whatever arose that was out of His order. He told them to take dominion over everything that moved on the earth. In this command, He was letting them know that they were in charge of keeping order.

When the serpent came, he began with a question about the Garden and the tree. When Eve confirmed with him that God had commanded them not to eat from it or even touch it because they'd surely die, Satan mocked the idea and contradicted God entirely. *"And the serpent said unto the woman,*

Ye shall not surely die: for God doth know that in the day ye eat thereof, then your eyes shall be opened, and ye shall be as gods, knowing good and evil" (Genesis 3:4-5).

Satan was appealing to Eve's pride. He was calling God a liar and putting God's motives into question. He was accusing God of being untruthful and withholding power from her. That should have made her subdue him and take dominion right there, but it didn't.

Now, just remember that the serpent didn't force the fruit in her mouth; all he did was talk. Satan is a master of deception, and it is always in opposition to God and what is actually good for mankind. Jesus called him a liar and the father of all lies (John 8:44). In our life, he often starts with a question, like he did with Eve—and it's all to sow doubt so that we will reject God, like he did, and so that we will see him as some great liberator. The moment you listen to him is the moment you play into his hand.

Well, Eve believed the lie of the "Light Bringer" and she told her husband, and he didn't step up and subdue the situation either. Instead, he went right along with the rebellion and ate the fruit, too. They both wanted the knowledge the Light Bringer told them they'd get, and they didn't believe the warning God had given them. They had no idea that the consequences were indeed going to happen exactly as God said. But in that choice to disobey, they confirmed to God that with their own free will they believed and sided with Satan—and so they got what they wanted, and a lot more that they didn't!

You can read about the full repercussions in Genesis 3, but essentially, when they both ate from the tree of knowledge of good and evil, they were immediately changed—they suddenly went from the "only-know-good" state of being they'd always known to the "know-both-good-and-evil" state of being that we all live under today. Their eyes were opened, they knew they were naked, and nothing was ever the same. The curse came upon them and they were driven out of the Garden.

It was actually mercy that God drove them out, because in that Garden was also the tree of life—the same tree that the Word also says is in Heaven—and it was this tree that kept them healthy, whole, and immortal. God knew that if they continued to stay and eat it, they'd live forever in their sinful state. The aging process began right then and there, and the march to death for their bodies began.

> *And the Lord God said, Behold, the man is become as one of us, to know good and evil: and now, lest he put forth his hand, and take also of the tree of life, and eat, and live for ever:*
>
> *Therefore the Lord God sent him forth from the garden of Eden, to till the ground from whence he was taken.*
>
> *So he drove out the man; and he placed at the east of the garden of Eden cherubims, and a flaming sword which turned every way, to keep the way of the tree of life.*
>
> GENESIS 3:22-24

Today, Satan is the ruler of this world (John 12:31). He commands the angels who rebelled along with him in Heaven, and they wreak havoc in the spiritual world, which directly affects our physical world. We all inherited the sin nature because of Adam and Eve, and without the redemption of sin and iniquity, we can be easily swayed to Satan's way of thinking, talking, and living.

Satan is still in opposition to God and us, and his demon legions do their best to sow strife between us and turn our hearts away from God—once you know this, though, it's easy to see the tactics. Ephesians 6:12 (NKJV) reveals that what influences and motivates people to do terrible things is spiritual: *"For we do not wrestle against flesh and blood, but against principalities, against powers, against the rulers of the darkness of this age, against spiritual hosts of wickedness in the heavenly places."*

I like to say principalities work through personalities, and that helps me not to fall into the trap of hate when I experience attacks or see what's going on in the world today—because according to that verse above, *principalities* are a category of Satan's fallen angels. *Powers* are too. There's an order to his rebellion. There are rulers of darkness that we know nothing about, but are orchestrating events here on earth.

There are fallen angels in leadership positions within Satan's war against God and mankind. There are even *spiritual hosts of wickedness*, and the scriptures tell us they are in heavenly places, which means the sky and beyond. There are evil angelic beings ruling over nations in this world, influencing flesh and blood people who lead. As I've mentioned, the prince of Persia and the prince of Greece are two specifically named in Daniel 10:13-20, but you can bet there are more.

The majority of the heavenly hosts who rebelled with Satan, mentioned in Revelation 12:4, are *not* rulers though—and you can find them everywhere in the scriptures and everywhere in our time, too. The same ones who wreaked havoc in the lives of people in biblical times didn't leave. I don't know if they're deluded, thinking that they're going to win this war, but they sure are giving it their best shot!

Of course, Satan and his fallen angels know what the Word of God says. They witnessed creation and every phase of man, including the writing of the Bible. They know God's Word says they'll lose in the end, but it doesn't seem to stop them. In their pride and lust for power and control, their minds have been corrupted. Whether they think they're going to win or they know the time is short and just want to get in as much stealing, killing, and destroying in before God's judgment on them comes to pass, I don't know. But I do know this: I've read the back of the Book and we win! There's only one place they are headed, and it is to a fiery eternal damnation.

So, what do we do as we go through this life when it comes to these fallen beings? Well, my whole ministry is dedicated to showing people how to receive Christ and live by the Word of God, and how to overcome every attack and obstacle Satan and his angels attempt. He may be a serial killer, but we serve a serial Savior—and we are more than conquerors through Him. Jesus changes *everything*, and He gives us the power to live completely opposite of Satan's way.

Satan's tactic is to always get us into fear because that is what is the opposite of faith. In Christ we gain *faith*—and faith blows fear away. Through the sacrificial work of Jesus on the cross, we gain *all* the power and authority we need to overcome the devil and all his evil works (1 John 5:1-5; Colossians 2:8-15; Ephesians 6:11). The scripture tells us how and it is simple. We are to *resist* the devil and he will flee (James 4:7)—like Jesus did, we are to resist him and just use the Word of God. It is the Word that is our weapon (Hebrews 4:12). It is our faith in the name of Jesus that we speak that gives us power over the enemy. We do everything in the power and authority Christ has given us, and we are to do nothing in our own strength.

We are never told to fight the devil. We cannot win if we try him; he's been here too long and our flesh can't compete. We win because Jesus already won, and we simply enforce Satan's defeat by speaking the Word of God in faith. That's why it's so important that we realize we are saved by grace through the blood of Jesus. That's why we must be confident in our salvation and all the power to overcome that it has given us.

As an accuser of the brethren, Satan and his fallen angels will always slyly try to guilt us about our past or our faults—if they can get us into thinking about ourselves and not Jesus, if they can get us to discount the redeeming blood of Jesus over our lives, they know they can weaken our faith. When we put more faith in what *we* did wrong than in the power of the blood to wash it away, we are walking right into the enemy's deception.

Never let the accuser make you feel guilty for what Jesus has redeemed you from—that is like agreeing with the devil that the blood doesn't matter. It does matter. There is no condemnation for those in Christ Jesus (Romans 8:1). The devil is just a liar and a thief trying to steal the faith out of your heart and the peace of God out of your life. There is no sin too bad for the blood to wash away. The blood of Jesus saves us completely. *"Therefore if any man be in Christ, he is a new creature; old things are passed away; behold, all things are become new"* (2 Corinthians 5:17). Notice that word "all." All means *all*.

We are never more than one breath away from being righteous in God's sight—because our repentance to God and acceptance of Jesus' sacrifice brings salvation, forgiveness, and pure righteousness in Christ. All we have to do is ask for forgiveness with a pure heart and the blood of Jesus comes rushing in, redeeming us from the hand of the enemy.

You see, when we know that all of our sins and iniquity have been washed in the blood, never to be remembered or held against us anymore, we can be bold in resisting the devil. Satan cannot cross the bloodline of Jesus Christ working in our lives, and neither can any demon. No matter what they try to do, all we have to do is speak the Word, stand firm on the power of Jesus' work at the cross, and RESIST them. If we resist, they will flee. They have to. They have no other choice.

Faith rids us of fear, whether it's fear of the devil or any of the works he and his legions of fallen angels do on the earth. Faith in God is the antidote to fleshly fear. Today, many people are living in fear, but God has called us to live in faith—it is a better way in every way!

There is an energetic force in faith that everything in the spirit understands—it's a mountain-moving substance that helps us to rise above what the fallen are doing and concentrate on what God has already done. When we *know* in Whom we have believed, like the apostle Paul said, we are walking by faith (2 Timothy 1:12). Faith is built only one way: by hearing, and hearing of the Word of God (Romans 10:17).

As believers living in a fallen world, we should never glorify Satan or his angels with admiration. We do not give them anything even near to praise. We do not admire their power. We do not fight them. We do not give attention to them or seek to engage them. We especially do not get into fear and worry about them. Our role as God's children is to do one thing: *RESIST* them, just like Jesus did in His earthly ministry. Again, I can't say it enough. If we resist the devil, he will flee. Period.

This has been a heavy chapter, but that's what evil brings: heaviness. Everything Satan does brings us down. But I want you to know this: life is not heavy when you serve the Lord in faith. In fact, it's a much lighter life with Jesus. His love, His joy, His peace . . . they lift the heart and make life wonderful. Satan may fight, but he can't win. God is on our side and His glorious, powerful angels are, too. They're hidden to us most of the time, but they are powerful workers and warriors on our behalf.

Jesus came to give us life, and life in abundance, regardless of the devil! Because of Jesus, we can go about our days with the strength of His joy—walking by faith, spreading the love of Jesus everywhere we go, and enjoying the life God has given us. We can help others find the Lord, and help and healing, too, through His Word. As believers, we are one big family— one family focused on living in Christ and spreading the word that with God, nothing is impossible . . . even living on a fallen planet with a bunch of demons running wild. They're no match for Jesus. They never were, and they never will be. And Jesus is Who lives in *you*. Don't forget it!

God is going to take care of the devil and every fallen being that's been in opposition to Him and to all that is good. Just wait. You'll see it with your own two eyes. One day all will be rectified through His just power. Until then, enjoy yourself and remember, there are more of God's angels still serving Him than the ones that got away. And, besides, God is a Creator. He can make more anytime He wants!

CHAPTER 16

THE WONDERFUL MINISTRY OF ANGELS IN THE LIFE, DEATH, AND RESURRECTION OF JESUS

"And without controversy great is the mystery of godliness: God was manifest in the flesh, justified in the Spirit, seen of angels, preached unto the Gentiles, believed on in the world, received up into glory."

1 TIMOTHY 3:16

"And He saith unto him, Verily, verily, I say unto you, Hereafter ye shall see Heaven open, and the angels of God ascending and descending upon the Son of Man."

JOHN 1:51

If you don't think of angels when you think of Jesus Christ, you haven't taken a look at the scriptures—because the angels of God are everywhere when it comes to Jesus. From His birth to His life, death, resurrection, and ascension into Heaven, angels follow the Lord. This is because Jesus was God manifest in the flesh, and God is always surrounded by angels. First Timothy 3:16, as mentioned above, sums it up best.

Jesus was God taking on a human form in order to save mankind from separation from Him. He was justified in the Spirit and seen of angels here on earth. Jesus was preached to those even outside of His covenant, and was believed on throughout the whole world. And after completing His redeeming work, He was received back into the glory of Heaven. When He said, *"It is finished"* on the cross, He meant it.

Satan may be the ruler of this world, but he no longer has the power and authority, and his days are numbered. He can't keep human beings blinded and spinning in sin and iniquity and without hope—because since the birth, death, and resurrection of Jesus, the price for our way back to God has been fully paid. All that *anyone* has to do now is make a draw on that sacrifice by calling upon the name of the Lord and accepting what He's done, and they can be saved. It doesn't matter who a person is or where they come from, salvation is available to the whole world.

> But what does it say? *"The word is near you, in your mouth and in your heart"(that is, the word of faith which we preach):*
> *That if you confess with your mouth the Lord Jesus and believe in your heart that God has raised Him from the dead, you will be saved.*
> *For with the heart one believes unto righteousness, and with the mouth confession is made unto salvation.*
> *For the Scripture says, "Whoever believes on Him will not be put to shame."*
> *For there is no distinction between Jew and Greek, for the same Lord over all is rich to all who call upon Him.*
> *For "whoever calls on the name of the Lord shall be saved."*
> ROMANS 10:8-13 NKJV

Where is Jesus today, now that His work here is finished? Today, Jesus is seated at the right hand of the Father, and the scripture says He's making intercession for all of us (Romans

8:34). He's praying. And He's also waiting . . . waiting for that moment when the Father decides enough is enough and He can come back for His Church. Jesus is coming! And if the past is any indication of the future, when He comes, angels will be celebrating once again.

Jesus and angels—it's hard to separate them when looking at His birth, life, and death. It seems like angels always played an important role in God coming to earth as a man. From the birth of Christ to His ascension, angels were there. If you think about it, God the Father is surrounded by angels in Heaven. It only stands to reason that they'd surround His Son here on earth, too.

One of my favorite quotes in the Bible from Jesus, talking about His power over angels, is after Judas betrayed Him with a kiss and a multitude of people came with clubs, swords, and with soldiers to violently take Him away. Peter took matters into his own hands and took out his own sword, cutting off the ear of one of those who got too close. Jesus picked up the ear, put it back on the man and totally healed him, and then turned to Peter and said, *"Put your sword in its place, for all who take the sword will perish by the sword. Or do you think that I cannot now pray to My Father, and He will provide Me with more than twelve legions of angels? How then could the Scriptures be fulfilled, that it must happen thus?"* (Matthew 26:52-54 NKJV)

You see, Jesus didn't need Peter's help to fight anybody. All He had to do was call on the Father to send Heaven's best warriors, and that would have been the end of that! It shows us how much power Jesus had and how close He was to God— that even in His humanity, all He had to do is make that call of prayer. The angels in Heaven would have been there in a split second.

He didn't even need angels, though, because power from the Father was given to Him over His very own life. I love when He said, "*Therefore My Father loves Me, because I lay down My life that I may take it again. No one takes it from Me, but I lay it down of Myself. I have power to lay it down, and I have power to take it again. This command I have received from My Father*" (John 10:17-18 NKJV).

Buddy, Jesus wasn't playing around! He was letting them know that He had the favor to call legions of angels and the gift to rise again—nobody could do anything to Jesus that He did not allow. He came here to fulfill God's plan. He knew He was destined to die for the sins of the world. Everything Jesus said and did was *on* purpose and for a purpose. Halleluiah! I get all stirred up just thinking about it! We don't serve some weakling. There's not a soul on earth or an angelic being anywhere that can hold a candle to His love for us or His power.

The wonderful presence of the angels of God was all around the Lord Jesus Christ. Let's look at some of the instances in the Word that confirm this glorious fact. Before Jesus was even born, Psalm 8:5 declared Him "*a little lower than the angels*" in most of the Bibles you read today—but the reality is that the word *angels* in this scripture isn't translated correctly. The original word is *Elohim*, another name for *God*.

I believe that the translators could not handle the idea that mankind and the Son of man, in their humanity, are "a little lower than God." It was likely sacrilegious to them because they had no real understanding of how it could be true. After all, human nature is weak by comparison to the powerfully strong angels God made. From the beginning of time until now, human beings have always thought of themselves as "lower" than angels because of their supernatural abilities. I don't believe this scripture is about ability, majesty, or power at all. I believe it's about what God originally created us to be, before sin entered in and degraded what He intended. We were created much differently than what you and I see in the world today. Still, this was His original plan. And while we may not live up to it now, after it's all said and done, we're going back to the way it always should have been—walking with God, like Adam, whole, at peace, and powerful . . . just a little lower than Elohim.

It was *God* Who established our place below Him, not fearful translators. So whenever you read that phrase *"a little lower than the angels,"* insert the word *God.* If it makes you flinch, remind yourself that you've been indoctrinated to believe that you're worth nothing—that you came from nothing, are expendable and replaceable, and that you don't really matter. This is a pure lie of Satan meant to undermine what God created in us.

God didn't send Himself as Christ to die for the angels who rebelled, but He did send Jesus to die for us when we rebelled. He didn't make us to be anything less than His family—beings made in *His* image and given the rank of a little lower than Elohim, which means Himself. When the devil tries to make you feel less than, just remember he's attacking the image of God—you're in the Family of God, and you just remind him of your Father!

Remind yourself Who your Father is when you are made to feel small. When the devil or anyone being motivated by him tries to discredit your value as God's child, just remind yourself that what you're hearing is a bold-faced lie. It's a lie from the father of all lies, who was defeated by Jesus and whose destiny is to be thrown in a lake of fire. That's *his* future. That's what God has chosen to do for *him.*

Your future is glorious because you're appointed unto grace and not unto wrath (1 Thessalonians 5:9). You are fearfully and wonderfully made (Psalms 139:14). You have Jesus Christ, the hope of glory, ruling and reigning in your life (Colossians 1:27). Don't let the devil make you think less of yourself than what God said about you—you're a little lower than Elohim, and that's how God made you. For millennia, the Church has not understood their position in Christ Jesus. It's almost not until these last days that we started to get it! Maybe that's how it was meant to be, I don't know. What I do know is that God is a good Father Who loves His children—He thinks we are worth the whole world, and He gave Himself to prove it (John 3:16).

God is moved with compassion for us because He knows what we're going through, because He experienced all the temptations and the emotions that go along with being human in a fallen world. When God took on human flesh, He also took on our frailty, our human nature, and was tempted in everything that we are tempted with. He felt what it was like to be us, in the flesh, and that's why the Word says that we don't have a Savior Who is unsympathetic to us (Hebrews 4:15). He knows first-hand what it means to be disparaged, forgotten, hurt, betrayed, stolen from, misunderstood, mistreated, lied about, abused, mocked, and even murdered.

When God decided to come to the earth as a man, He came with our salvation on His mind—and angels helped those who would raise Him as an earthly man, knowing He was coming. Angels were a part of Jesus' earthly life. Mary, the mother of God, and later Joseph, her betrothed, were both visited by *angels*. God let them know their Son would be different and a Savior for humanity (Luke 1:26-38, Matthew 1:20-23). When Jesus was born, angels announced it to shepherds tending their fields nearby, and the sky lit up with a multitude of *angels* singing in celebration and proclamations (Luke 2:8-21).

When Jesus was under two years old, *angels* protected Him from King Herod's murderous decree to kill all the boys two and under by directing Joseph to flee to Egypt (Matthew 2:13-15).

When Jesus was led by the Spirit of God into the wilderness to be tempted by the devil, it was *angels* who came to minister to Him after He refused to fall into the devil's traps (Matthew 4:1-11).

When Jesus knew He was about to go to the cross and wrestling with the upcoming pain and suffering of the cross, it was an *angel* who came to strengthen Him for the pain and torture—both physically and spiritually—that lay just ahead (Luke 22:39-43).

When Jesus rose from the dead and left the tomb, it was an *angel* from Heaven who came and rolled back the stone from the door—and sat on it, to show that Jesus was gone and to proclaim that He had risen. As you know, I love this story. To me, Christianity was born at this moment and the first evangelists were women, both scared and full of joy as they ran from the empty tomb with the message that He had risen. Jesus Himself interrupted them along the way to tell them, "Rejoice!" and to go tell the others He'd meet them too from beyond the grave, in Galilee. Glory! Go read this whole story again (Matthew 28). It'll bless you!

When Jesus spoke His last words on earth to His disciples before ascending into Heaven with a cloud receiving Him out of sight, His disciples were dumbfounded. They stared into the sky, unable to move, and it was two men in white clothes, *angels* in disguise, who brought them to their senses again, saying, *"why do you stand gazing up into Heaven? This same Jesus, Who was taken from you into Heaven will so come in like manner as you saw Him go into Heaven"* (Acts 1:9-11 NKJV). Glory! We have the return of Jesus to look forward to, and as I've said, I believe it's sooner than we think!

When Jesus returns to this earth, He promised that we would physically see Him coming *"in the glory of His Father with His angels"* (Matthew 16:27).

And, finally, when Jesus comes back to take us with Him, we will know it when we hear the shout of an archangel and the trumpet of God. *"For the Lord Himself will descend from Heaven with a shout, with the voice of an archangel, and with the trumpet of God. And the dead in Christ will rise first. Then we who are alive and remain shall be caught up together with them in the clouds to meet the Lord in the air. And thus we shall always be with the Lord. Therefore comfort one another with these words"* (1 Thessalonians 4:16-18).

We have an amazing future, and we can have an amazing life here and now, too. God's angels are everywhere in the Bible—these highlights are just some of the things they've done for Jesus. But in every good work He did in His earthly ministry, there is no reason to believe that angels weren't there helping. They help to draw people to Christ now, after His finished work. So there's no good reason to think they didn't help then, too.

Even fallen angels saw Jesus Christ during His ministry and acknowledged His lordship (Matthew 8:28-32; Mark 1:23-26, 5:1-15; Luke 4:33-37, 8:26-36). And do you know why? It's because both God's angels and Satan's angels see everything—and they recognize the power of Almighty God on a person's life. They recognize when God's Spirit and God's anointing are flowing in a person, and it gets their attention.

Well, I could spend a lifetime writing about Jesus—this is just a little bit to show you how angels surrounded His life, and how they are surrounding all of us believers, too. I'll leave you with one amazing scene from Revelation 5:11-13, where it prophesies a time when over 100,000,000 angels will declare in one loud voice that Jesus, the Lamb slain for you and me, is worthy of *all* power, riches, wisdom, strength, honor, glory, and blessing.

Then, after the angels speak with one voice, *every creature*—whether they are in Heaven, on earth, under the earth, or even in the sea—will also unite to declare that *all* blessing, honor, glory, and power belong to God, Who sits on the throne, and to the Lamb, His Son, Jesus, forever and ever!

I don't know about you, but that paints a perfect picture of both of our worlds in spiritual unity to me. Can you imagine it? Every knee bowing and every tongue confessing that *Jesus* is Lord. Can you see it? The chasm closing and both the spiritual and the natural world coming together in unity. Everything, everywhere, *all* of God's creation in Heaven and Earth coming together to honor, glorify, and praise both the Lamb and the One Who became Him: our wonderful, majestic, and creative Father: GOD.

One day soon, I believe you won't have to imagine it at all. You'll be living it, side by side with the angels, giving praise to His holy name. Get that picture in your mind, because one day it's going to be your reality.

CHAPTER 17

THE ANOINTING DRAWS ANGELIC ATTENTION: ANGELS IN THE CHOIR LOFT

I was ministering in a small church in a town called Mer Rouge, Louisiana many years ago. It's a small town above Monroe and Bastrop, and not very well known. The year was either 1979 or 1980, I can't remember which, but I do remember it was a Tuesday night and the sanctuary was packed. I've told this story before many times, but I felt led to share it in this book— because it really blew me away.

Now, this church had a pretty starchy group of people both running it and attending it. They were denominational and not interested in anything "charismatic." I was such a young preacher then and I flowed in the gifts of the Spirit regularly. I was considered, by all accounts, a charismatic preacher. I really don't know why they invited me to preach for them in the first place! For many years I've been able to cross Christian denominational barriers pretty easily. I've been so blessed in that area all throughout my ministry. I think it's the humor and because most people know I'm not mean-spirited about what I believe.

My take is that if someone doesn't believe the same as I do in some areas of the faith, it's OK. I'm not God. I'm not their judge. We're all learning and on a journey with God, and besides that, I find that there are always more things I can find to agree on than to disagree on. I like talking to people about what I believe, but I don't want to fight about God at all! How will people know we are disciples of Christ? They'll know by the love we have for one another (John 13:35).

Since this church I'd been invited to wasn't charismatic, I had planned to simply preach that night and not to move in the gifts of the Spirit. As a guest, I didn't want to offend them. Anyway, I sang along in the congregation during their song service time and when it was time for me to speak, the pastor introduced me and I made my way to the pulpit. I opened my Bible and started to preach on what the Lord had given me for them.

Now, I believe the Word of God itself is anointed. Every Word that comes from God has an energy and power—and when it's spoken in faith and people are open to hear it in faith, things often shift in the spirit realm that are easy to feel. Well, that night, the anointing of God fell on me as I preached, and I found myself just shouting and sweating, with the words coming out of my spirit like a speeding train. I was flowing and I could feel the energy of faith on the Word.

Back then, I was young and talked fast. But that night? I was on fire! I felt like I wasn't even in charge of my mouth, and the words were just flying out of my spirit to those people. I can't even remember what point I was sharing, but at some point in that sermon, whatever came out of my spirit shook me to my shoes. I shut my eyes, I turned around and clenched my fists tight with my back to the people, and I remember saying, "Well alright!!!" My back was to the crowd when I opened my eyes and I was about to turn around, but what I saw stopped me cold.

Up in the choir loft area, there were these massive, long shafts of bright white light. I could see them. I stood totally dumbfounded. I couldn't say anything, not a word. I was just shocked because I knew that I was looking at a choir loft full of angels. The light coming off of them was so bright and so intense that it was difficult to even see their features at all. These HUGE shafts of white light were literally beaming off of the center of their forms. The light was like rays going in every direction. To top it off, as I looked at them, I could see that each one was focused on *me*. I could hardly believe my eyes. It was like the angels were kicking back in the choir loft listening to the sermon! I knew they were watching me preach.

For a short time, I stood with my back to the people in silence staring into that choir loft in utter amazement. The congregation was silent too, and I think they were probably wondering what was going on and why I was looking at the choir loft and the back wall instead of preaching to them. Finally I just muttered, "Whoa." I know it sounds dumb, but that's all I could get out. When I said that, a lady sitting in the back of the church jumped to her feet and screamed out, "I see them, too!" I turned around to the congregation to see the lady and she was staring with wide eyes and pointing her finger to the choir loft at the angels. She could see what I saw, and she was the only other one that could.

I turned back around and, suddenly, in one motion, the angels all stood to their feet—and they walked through the choir loft. I don't mean they went single-file out the row, but they actually stepped *through* it, like it wasn't a solid material. It was like matter itself didn't affect them. The wood of the loft was nothing to them and they could pass right through it, and they did. The sight of them was so incredible and majestic that all I could do was stare in awe. As I watched these huge, gleaming angels walk towards the congregation, one of them in the first row turned his face towards me—and I could see his features, and he looked at me and smiled. I was fixated on him and I watched him walk right past me. And then I looked into the face of the one right behind him. It was like they were revealing themselves to me, while the rest were just like moving light.

It was then that I began to notice what was happening in the congregation, because these angels began walking straight through the people sitting in the pews. And as they did, pews full of people began to be affected. I could see the people acting as if they were in a prayer line with hands being laid on them—they were falling out in the Spirit, so to speak, and it was happening all at once! Still, I could say nothing, and the lady who could also see them was dumbstruck, too.

As those angels continued to walk, going straight through the sanctuary towards the back doors, I saw pews of people just bite the dust right where they were sitting! Pew after pew, the angels continued to walk through the people until eventually they disappeared out the back wall and doors of the church.

At that point, I looked at the congregation and from where I was standing, it looked like everyone in the building had been affected by those angels—they'd fallen out in the Spirit and were either out cold or groggy. Some were on the ground, others were sprawled out all over the pews, and others had fallen sideways into the aisles! I knew there had to be sinners in that place and not just the righteous, and I guess even they had fallen out under the power of those beings. It looked like an altar call had happened and the whole church had hands laid on them and were out in the Spirit!

With everybody knocked out, I didn't have anyone to preach to, so I just sat down. What else could I do? And from where I was sitting on the platform, I could see people starting to move and get themselves together. Most were getting back to sitting up straight, but some were trying to get down the aisles towards the back doors, like they wanted to leave. They were trying to get out of that church! Later, someone told me that they'd found a man who had been in the foyer on his knees, crawling around, and trying to find the door. He kept saying, "I'm not into this stuff, just let me out!"

The funny part is that the pastor of the church didn't believe in falling out in the Spirit—he didn't believe that stuff at all. In fact, he taught against it! And there he and his wife were, laid right out on the front pew. They'd fallen out in the Spirit along with the rest of their congregation. Finally, most of the people were up and settled, but because hardly any of them had experienced the power of God in any tangible way before, they all began to chatter and, soon, people were just sharing what they had felt. Everyone seemed to testify to just about the same feeling. As one farmer put it, "I suddenly lost all my strength. I couldn't even stand up!" It was a miracle and a breakthrough for that church concerning supernatural things.

However, I found it interesting that while only two people in the church actually saw the angels, the whole congregation felt the power of them. I think God was trying to get something over to that pastor and that congregation. I believe that He gave two witnesses to say what happened, but ultimately, I think God was trying to say, "Look, people, I'm here in your midst whether you see Me or not!" Faith doesn't come by what you see. You can see something and not even believe your own eyes. Faith comes by hearing, and hearing by the Word of God. When faith and the Word mix, anointing comes. That's an energy and a force that is God-created—and His angelic beings facilitate that.

I want you to know that the Lord is in your midst every day whether you see Him or not. You don't have to understand everything God is or does to believe in His power—and you shouldn't have to see to believe. This life is a vapor. The angelic realm lives in a dimension we can't see with the naked eye—and it's up to God or them if they choose to lift the veil and reveal themselves to us. The angels of God are meant to be hidden forces at work in this world.

There are things happening in the spirit realm that you may never see. You may not understand it, and that's OK. You don't have to understand everything God does. The important thing is that you recognize that He's God and His ways are higher than all of your ways—and that you have faith in Him, knowing that what you see today is not all there is.

We see as *"through a glass, darkly"* when it comes to what's going on in this earth, as the scripture says (1 Corinthians 13:12). One day, *all* will be revealed. One day, there will be no barrier between the spiritual and the natural. Until then, we just have to remember that God is true and God is real. He's always with us whether we see Him or not . . . and guess what? His angels are, too.

Never forget that God's anointing rests on His Word and it really doesn't matter who speaks it. I'm a Cajun who loves God, that's it. Back then, I was so young in the ministry and I had a lot further to go in life. But I had a love for God and a faith in His Word that I could barely contain. And that night, it was like it was coming out of my pores!

I've learned that sincere love for God and real, childlike faith in His Word change everything. They charge the atmosphere with anointing—and the anointing really draws angelic attention. God's angels are always listening for His Word. And they go to work on our behalf when we use that Word and speak it out from the heart with a true belief that what God said, He meant . . . and what God said, He will do.

Did that experience with angels so long ago give me more faith? No. I was just as on fire for God before I saw a choir loft full of them as I was after. But I think that's how it should be, and who knows? Maybe that's one reason why they showed up. Never underestimate the power of your faith or its effect on the Hidden Help. I found out that they love God's Word so much, they'll even show up to hear a human preach it!

I hope you enjoyed *The Hidden Help*. They're here, you know, whether you see them or not. So, give God your best. Dwell in His presence and soak up His Word. Do right by God by loving not only Him but your fellow man too, as you go through life. After all, you really never know if you are *"entertaining angels unawares."*

—*Jesse Duplantis*

PRAYER OF SALVATION

"For God so loved the world, that He gave His only begotten Son, that whosoever believeth in Him should not perish, but have everlasting life. For God sent not His Son into the world to condemn the world; but that the world through Him might be saved."

JOHN 3:16-17

Do you know my Jesus? If you've never prayed a prayer of salvation, or if you just need to come back home to God where you belong, would you take a moment and pray with me today? This prayer below is a guide, but feel free to talk to God from your heart. Wherever you are right now, no matter what your situation, be sincere and God will meet you where you are—He will hear your prayer, loose the chains of sin off of your soul, and set you free with the blood of His precious Son, Jesus. If you are ready to start new, leave old things behind, and begin your personal relationship with the Lord, pray this with me now:

"God, thank You for loving me enough to send Your Son for my sins. I know that I need You. I believe that You are my God, my Maker, and my Father—and I believe that You sent Your only begotten Son to pay the price for sin and to redeem all who accept Your plan. I accept Your plan of salvation through the death and resurrection of Jesus right now, God. Like all, I know I've sinned and fallen short, and

I need help. Jesus, come into my life right now. Wash my sins away and create a new heart in me now. Thank You for paying the price for me on the cross. Thank You for drawing me to You and opening my eyes to the truth. From this point on, I will seek Your will and ways for my life. I will talk to You every day and make Your Word the light that guides my life. I want to find my best life in You. Thank You, Jesus! I know Your favor will surround me and Your blessings will follow me all the days of my life, and Heaven will be my eternal home. Thank You for loving me enough to give Yourself, and for continuing to help me in every area of my life as I turn to you each day."

If you have prayed this prayer, you are in the Family of God. It wasn't hard, was it? People sometimes make things hard, but because of Jesus, salvation is easy. I'm your brother in the faith now, along with millions of others all around the world who have accepted God's plan of salvation. Isn't that amazing? We will all have eternity together, but for now, your aim is to grow in your faith and relationship with the Lord. Read your Bible daily for wisdom. Listen to messages that will encourage your faith as often as you can. Find a church to attend regularly. Being with others of like precious faith is so important, and God has so much in store for you as you follow Him—new people, new ideas about how to live well, and new insights for your own journey in life. Welcome to the family, and may God bless you as you go and grow!

—*Jesse Duplantis*

ABOUT THE AUTHOR

Jesse Duplantis, minister of the Gospel, motivational speaker, television personality, and best-selling author, has been in full-time ministry since 1978 and is the founder of Jesse Duplantis Ministries, located in the Greater New Orleans area of south Louisiana in the United States of America. With over four decades of sharing his unique blend of humor and faith around the world, generations of believers have been inspired by his messages, and countless numbers have come to know Jesus Christ as Savior through his ministry.

Known for his unflinching, status-quo-breaking messages, and humorous take on experiences in the life of the believer, Jesse continues to draw large audiences of believers through social media, television, and meetings held around the world. With speaking engagements booked years in advance, Jesse Duplantis continues to keep an intense traveling schedule, flying throughout the United States and the world preaching the Gospel of Jesus Christ. With no booking agents pursuing meetings for him and no set fees imposed upon churches for speaking engagements, Jesse chooses his outreach meetings based on the same two criteria he always has: invitations that come in and prayer over each one. This uncommon way of scheduling in today's world means Jesse's many followers may find him speaking in some of the largest churches and venues in America and the world, as well as a great many small and growing congregations, too. No church is too big or small for the Holy Spirit, as he says.

Side by side with his wife Cathy Duplantis, the co-founder and chief of staff of Jesse Duplantis Ministries and the senior pastor of Covenant Church in Destrehan, Louisiana, Jesse continues to fulfill his life's calling by daily taking up the Great Commission of Jesus Christ: *"Go ye into all the world, and preach the Gospel to every creature"* (Mark 16:15). Through social media, television broadcasts, books, and other ministry products, as well as through many evangelistic meetings, the JDM website, the JDM App, and *Voice of the Covenant* magazine, Jesse Duplantis continues to see growth in his ministry and expand each year while maintaining his roots. Jesus is the center of his life. The salvation of lost people and the growth of believers is the purpose of his ministry. And for both he and his wife, every day is another day to *"Reach People and Change Lives, One Soul at a Time."*

OTHER BOOKS

by Jesse Duplantis

I Never Learned to Doubt
The Lessons I've Learned about the Dangers of Doubt and the Freedom of Faith

The Most Wonderful Time of the Year
Uncommon Lessons from the Christmas Story

Your Everything Is His Anything
Expand Your View of What Prayer and Faith Can Do

Advance in Life
From Revelation to Inspiration to Manifestation

The Big 12
My Personal Confidence-Building Principles for Achieving Total Success

Living at the Top
How to Prosper God's Way and Avoid the Pitfalls of Success

For by IT . . . FAITH
If You Don't Know What "IT" Is, You Won't Have It!

DISTORTION
The Vanity of Genetically Altered Christianity

The Everyday Visionary
Focus Your Thoughts, Change Your Life

What in Hell Do You Want?

Wanting a God You Can Talk To

Jambalaya for the Soul
Humorous Stories and Cajun Recipes from the Bayou

Breaking the Power of Natural Law
Finding Freedom in the Presence of God

God Is Not Enough, He's Too Much!
How God's Abundant Nature Can Revolutionize Your Life

Heaven
Close Encounters of the God Kind

The Ministry of Cheerfulness

OTHER CONTENT

Other ministry resources by Jesse Duplantis are available through www.jdm.org and the JDM App (Total.JDM.org).

CONTACT US

To contact Jesse Duplantis Ministries with prayer requests, praise reports, comments, or to schedule Jesse Duplantis at your church, conference, or seminar, please write, call, or email:

Jesse Duplantis Ministries
PO Box 1089
Destrehan, LA 70047
985-764-2000
www.jdm.org

We also invite you to connect with us on social media:

Facebook:	/JesseDuplantisMinistries
Twitter:	@jesse_duplantis
Instagram:	@jesseduplantisministries
YouTube:	/jesseduplantisministries
Pinterest:	/JesseDuplantisMinistries
TikTok:	@jesseduplantisministries

Made in the USA
Middletown, DE
03 April 2023